Student Teaching Handbook

Dear Authors

'We Convert Fighters into Writers'. That's our main motto. Our message to the world is that India can win the battle not only by the bullet but also by the pen. There is no dearth of intellectuals in our country, but their knowledge is confined to them only. No sincere effort has been made by any other publisher to channelise their knowledge in national interest. That is why the talent of a large number of intellectuals remains latent. An author transforms his knowledge into a manuscript, and it is our job to spread his/her knowledge by converting it into a beautiful book. For over four decades, We are motivating the intellectuals by publishing their manuscripts and would like to publish your manuscript too. If you or your colleagues have any manuscript ready for publication or are working on it, kindly contact us with detailed synopsis and list of contents. We will transform your work into a valuable publication. If you wish, we can also suggest you the suitable subjects for writing the books related to your area of expertise. We are known for its publishing quality and commitments. We take utmost care in production and give wide publicity to the book as well as its author through our national and international distribution network.

Student Teaching Handbook

Daniel K Thompson

Books for Libraries
Delhi-110042

Books for Libraries

B-420, Shahbad Daulatpur,
Near Vikram, Dharam Kanta
Delhi-110042
Ph: 9212268682
E-mail: books for libraries@hotmail.com

Daniel K. Thompson

2016

ISBN 978-81-926482-6-2
₹ 495/-

Designed at
Books for Libraries

Printed in India at
R.K. Print Services, Delhi
and published by Mrs Rekha Garg,
Books for Libraries, B-420, Shahbad Daulatpur,
Near Vikram Dharam Kanta,
Delhi-110042 (INDIA)

Contents

Part 4 Appendices

Preface

This Handbook is designed to be helpful to all of you involved in the student teaching experience–student teachers, mentor teachers and university supervisors. Because each member of the triad plays a vital role in creating the best possible experience, information is included to insure that all of you have congruent expectations for assignments, roles, policies and assessment procedures. Throughout the Handbook, the student teacher is addressed as "you," in our attempt to make it a personal communication as well as a guide.

The student teaching semester is one of the most challenging and rewarding components of the teacher education program at Penn State. As the capstone experience of the teacher preparation program, the student teaching practicum provides you with exceptional opportunities to make a difference in the social, emotional, and intellectual lives of students. The student teaching journey will take you down many paths of joy, anxiety, wonder, and excitement. Because student teaching can be stressful as well as rewarding, it is important to be well organized, eat well, and get enough sleep in order to be alert and focused.

Each of you will be mentored and guided on this journey by an experienced classroom teacher and a supportive university-based faculty member who will serve as your supervisor. The university supervisor will provide you with a course syllabus detailing the specific requirements for each particular practicum. You are to read both the handbook and the syllabus carefully, share them with the mentor teacher, and refer to them often. Best wishes for a successful, student teaching experience.

Daniel K Thompson

Chapter 1

Student Teaching Program

1.1 Definition of Student Teaching

Student Teaching is a full-semester, full-time, full-day, clinical component of the teacher preparation program for Penn State students seeking initial teacher certification. The primary purpose of the student teaching experience is to provide you with a carefully mentored experience to help you develop and enhance the knowledge, skills, and dispositions necessary to positively impact student learning and development.

Field experiences such as student teaching are cooperative endeavors in which host schools work closely with the University to provide quality experiences for teacher certification candidates. Hosting a student teacher is a major professional commitment by teachers, administrators, and school boards. The university faculty supervisor and mentor teacher provide intense, supportive guidance to help you learn and enhance your professional role. Other school personnel, such as principals and department heads, also play a crucial role in mentoring you. All of these will be working together to help you become the best teacher you can be.

1.2 Teacher Education Performance Framework

A framework that specifies the understandings, abilities, and dispositions that should be demonstrated by new teachers guides the Penn State teacher preparation programs and the student teaching experience. Penn State student teachers in the early childhood and elementary program and those in the secondary and world language education programs are expected to develop proficiency in the following areas:

- Planning and Preparing for Student Learning
- Teaching
- Analyzing Student Learning and Inquiry into Teaching, and
- Fulfilling Professional Responsibilities.

A copy of this framework can be found in Appendix A. of this handbook.

1.3 Your Responsibilities as the Student Teacher

Because student teaching is a full-semester, full-time, full-day clinical experience, it requires full commitment and dedication from you. **No other coursework is permitted, and you are discouraged from holding jobs in order to have sufficient time for full participation as well as planning, preparation, and reflection.** It is expected that you will participate in non-instructional duties such as before- and after-school meetings, bus duty, lunch duty, and other extra curricular activities deemed appropriate by the mentor teacher and university supervisor. Some specific responsibilities include:

Being a Good Communicator: You need to actively listen

and communicate with the mentor teacher and the university supervisor. It is expected that honest and tactful discussion and reflection on experiences, accomplishments, and areas for improvement will occur, especially during the midterm and final assessment conferences.

Being Committed: You need to show initiative and commitment to both the students in the classroom and to your own work as a learner of teaching. You need to observe carefully to learn procedures and should volunteer for duties that you can handle, especially housekeeping duties and routine non-instructional tasks.

Being Prepared: You must always be prepared to fulfill any and all expectations and obligations, with the promptly at school each day and remain until the mentor teacher is scheduled to leave the school.

Being Responsible: There are many tasks, assignments, and types of paperwork associated with student teaching. You must familiarize yourself with the expectations that you will be held to and complete all tasks to the best of your abilities. Maintaining a highly organized and accessible filing system to keep track of all paperwork and assignments will facilitate successful completion of assignments.

By the start of the practicum you should have established an active eCredentials file with Penn State Career Services. **It is your responsibility to activate the file by contacting the Career Services Office at: (814-865-5131) in 105 Bank of America Bldg., University Park, PA 16802.** (http://www.sa.psu.edu/career/)

Acting Professionally: You communicate much about yourself through appearance, language, and behavior. Professional appearance and behavior allow you to establish credibility more easily with students, parents, and teaching colleagues.

Inquiring Thoughtfully: You are learning to teach.

Learning is an act of inquiry best supported by careful observations and thoughtful analyses. You are encouraged to formulate questions and seek answers in order to improve your understandings and abilities to support the learning and development of all students. The mentor teacher and the university supervisor are available to support and guide you throughout this experience. Please do not hesitate to ask them for assistance.

1.4 Responsiblities of the University Supervisor

The university supervisor is a faculty member of Penn State's College of Education and has full-time supervision responsibilities. Because she or he resides in the general vicinity of the student teaching placements, the supervisor is readily available to you and school personnel for consultation and assistance.

As a liaison between schools and the University, the supervisor builds and maintains collaborative relationships among University and school district personnel that insure optimal opportunities for learning to teach. The supervisor is in regular e-mail and phone communication with faculty at University Park. In addition, he or she attends regularly scheduled meetings at the University Park Campus each semester.

On your behalf, the University Supervisor engages in the following practices before, during, and after the practicum:

Prior to Student Teaching

University Park Interviews: During the semester prior to student teaching, prospective student teachers and university supervisors meet for the first time. Information is collected and reviewed to help the supervisor find a suitable placement for you. Only general information about the regional assignment is shared, as specific placements haven't been made at this point.

Procuring School Placements: Each university

supervisor, in compliance with individual school district protocol, seeks and procures specific school placements for each student teacher assigned to her/his cohort. Mentor teachers must be recommended by building principals and approved by school boards.

University Park Orientation: Each university supervisor conducts an orientation session at the University Park campus during the latter part of the semester preceding student teaching. At this orientation, your supervisor will provide you with information about your specific school placement, housing, transportation, important dates and other pertinent details.

Orientation in the Field: At the beginning of the student teaching practicum, each university supervisor conducts an orientation session for her/his cohort at a location central to the school placement sites. In this orientation, your supervisor will detail program requirements and expectations and help you complete administrative tasks.

Mentor teacher Orientations: Prior to and/ or during the first week of student teaching, the university supervisor provides practicum orientation for mentor teachers to ensure a collaborative process for merging school and University curricula and expectations.

During the Practicum

One of the benefits of having full-time supervising faculty is the opportunity for frequent observations and conferences with each of you throughout the student teaching experience. The observation-conference-goal setting cycle is critical to your progress and ongoing professional development. The role of the supervisor includes:

Observing Performance: The university supervisor observes you in a variety of teaching-learning situations on a regular basis during the student teaching experience. The observation records are used as a basis for helping you to analyze the teaching-learning process. Conferencing: Direct and regular feedback is provided through different types of conferences.

Initial Conference: The supervisor holds an initial conference during the first week of student teaching to discuss adjustments to the student teaching practicum.

Post-Observation Conference: The supervisor conducts a conference as soon as possible after a teaching observation. Three-way conferences, which include the mentor teacher, are scheduled when appropriate. Observation data are used to help identify appropriate goals for change and improvement. Self-evaluation is stressed to help you understand the impact of teaching behaviors upon students' learning and development.

Mid-Semester Conference: The supervisor schedules a three-way conference (student teacher, mentor teacher, university supervisor) near the midpoint in the semester. The purpose of this conference is to review evidence about your performance at this stage.

You will be asked to provide evidence of your accomplishments in each domain and participate in setting goals for the rest of the experience. This evidence is also part of your portfolio conference held mid-way through the semester.

Final Conference: A final three-way assessment conference is scheduled near the end of the student teaching experience. You will be required to present evidence demonstrating the extent to which you have accomplished each of the standards of the Performance-based Assessment. Mid-semester goals will also be reviewed to determine achievement in the areas targeted for growth.

General Conferences: Two-way and three-way conferences are held as the need arises throughout the semester to help you become the most effective teacher you can become.

Weekly Seminars: The university supervisor plans and conducts weekly seminars that focus on your needs and concerns, as well as current educational issues. Topics will include assessment, classroom management, instructional strategies, differentiated instruction, special education topics, educational law, etc.

Resource for Mentor teacher: Throughout the practicum, the supervisor acts as a resource for mentor teachers to assist them in their role as mentors.

After the Practicum

The university supervisor ensures that practicum grade(s), the student teaching cumulative file, and final assessments completed by the supervisor and mentor teacher are filed appropriately with the University. Thanking the mentor teacher and the school district for hosting you is also done at this time.

Supervisor Responsibilities for Short-term Student Teaching Abroad 2012-2013

1. The U.S. student teaching supervisor will complete a PDE 430 at the mid- point of the semester and a final PDE 430 at the end of the U.S. experience.
2. The U.S. student teaching supervisor, mentor and student will complete ST-1 assessments and participate in conferences at the mid-point and at the end of the U.S. experience.
3. In order to leave the U.S. placement and go abroad, the student teacher's performance must warrant at least a satisfactory rating at the end of the U.S. experience. The U.S. supervisor will give the final performance rating with consultation from the mentor. (Students are required to purchase trip insurance so that they will not forfeit the travel money if they are not able to go to the host nation placement.)
4. At the end of the U.S. experience, elementary

supervisors will recommend a grade for CI 495D based on the student teacher's performance to date.

5. While at the host nation school, the student teacher will send weekly journals via email to the U.S supervisor from the list of suggested topics (see Required Assignments). The student teacher will also complete the Final Performance Framework Portfolio Assignment and will submit it to the supervisor for evaluation through Taskstream.
6. At the end of student teaching, elementary student teaching supervisors will assign a grade for CI 495F while secondary student teaching supervisors will recommend a grade for CI 495E that is based on performance in the classroom in the U.S. as well as the required student teaching assignments, submission of weekly journals, final portfolio.
7. The Elementary CIFE Coordinator, Secondary CIFE Coordinator, and the Professor in Charge of CIFE will assign the final grade for CI 495D or CI 495E based on the supervisor's recommendation and information about the student teacher's performance abroad.
8. U.S. supervisors, international supervisors, and mentor teachers will write letters of reference for the student teacher using the eCredentials process.The student teacher will also complete the Final Performance Framework Portfolio. The student teacher will need to request the letters through eCredentials.

Suggested Schedule[A] - Short Team Student Teaching Abroad

1	Fall	Spring
US Placement Start after	Week before or week of Labor Day	First day of school New Years
US Palcement End	At 12 weeks	At 12 weeks
Number of weeks in Us		12 12
Number of In'I weeks	5	5
week 1	Observing, assisting and	Observing, assisting and
week 2-3	Planning and teaching[B] 1 to	Planning and teaching[B] 1to
week 4-5	40-60% of teaching and planning responsibilities	40-60 % of teaching and planning responsibilities.
week 6	Mid-term Conference First PDE 430 completed First St-1 completed	Mid-term Conference First PDE 430 completed First St-1 completed.
week 7-8	75-90% of planning and teaching responsibilities	75-90% of planning and teaching responsibilities.
week 9-11	Full time planning and teaching responsibilities	Full time planning and teaching responsibilities.
week 12 Last week in U.S. Placement	Final Conference Final ST-1 completed 2nd PDE 430 completed	Final Conference Final St-1 completed 2nd PDE 430 completed.

[A]Supervisors and mentors always have the discretion to match the suggested schedule to the student teaching context and the student teacher's capabilities.

[B]We expect student teachers to become capable of teaching independently during the student teaching experience. That said, co-teaching with the mentor teacher is preferred as a model of teaching whenever possible since it has the potential to benefit P-12 students. In addition to co-teaching, the student teacher should experience some solo teaching.

1.5 Role of the Mentor Teacher

The mentor teacher, an essential person in your practicum experience, exerts a powerful influence over your values, attitudes and practices. The mentor begins by setting the stage so that the classroom environment is favorable to your success and then provides on-going guidance. In accepting a student teacher as another professional in the classroom, the mentor will be sharing planning and teaching responsibilities with you. The mentoring relationship seeks the delicate balance between modeling his or her own practices, and affording opportunities for development of your potential. The mentor's role involves the following:

Welcoming You to the Classroom

Prior to and during the first few weeks of student teaching, the mentor teacher can help you adjust to the school setting in some of the following ways:

- Helping you become acquainted with the student teaching requirements.
- Informing the students that there will be another teacher in the room. This helps both you and the classroom students adjust to the new situation.
- Conversing informally in order to get to know you as an individual.
- Making introductions to faculty and other school personnel.
- Providing you with a work area and a space for personal belongings; and making available copies of student texts, teacher's editions, district curriculum guidelines, etc.
- Acquainting you with instructional supplies, teaching aids, and available equipment (e.g., audio-visual equipment, computer hardware and software, copying machines).
- Encouraging you to learn the names of the students as quickly as possible.

- Helping you to become acquainted with people in the community.
- Sensitizing you to the community and its educational resources.
- Familiarizing you with district policies and procedures.

Enhancing Observation and Participation

Early in the practicum, you will be observing carefully. The mentor teacher can provide assistance with effective observation and comfortable participation by doing the following:

- Encouraging you to observe with a purpose. Suggested foci include how lessons are introduced and closed, strategies to maintain students' interest and management techniques.
- Providing opportunities to observe and study classroom routines, procedures and rules.
- Introducing you to classroom management styles and teaching procedures, and discussing different ways to handle problems.
- Encouraging involvement in preparation and discussion of daily and long-term planning, including assessment and record keeping techniques.
- Inviting you to participate in activities that will build confidence, generate interaction with pupils, and acquire organizational skills (e.g., taking roll, administering tests, reading aloud, giving individual help to students, grading papers and recording grades).
- Involving you in school meetings.
- Appropriately including you in conferences with parents.
- Familiarizing you with routine classroom duties apart from preparing and implementing lessons.
- Introducing you to record-keeping procedures and practices.
- Utilizing a variety of observation techniques and sharing the data collected with you.

Providing Support as You Move into a Full-time

Teaching Role

By the end of the practicum, you will be expected to experience all aspects of full-time teaching responsibilities. Throughout the experience, the mentor teacher will be available to provide support, suggestions, alternatives, and guidelines.

Supervising Performance

A key component of success in student teaching is the quality of the daily supervision. High quality supervision includes all of the following actions:

- Observing on a regular basis and in a variety of situations.
- Providing feedback on the performance of professional responsibilities (lesson planning, implementation and assessment, classroom interaction, maintenance of records).
- Including both positive and negative perceptions of performance.
- Helping relate teaching theory to teaching in the classroom (e.g., reasons for selection of certain instructional materials and methods).
- Identifying the ways in which basic principles of learning are applied.
- Encouraging good preparation and organization by requiring all lesson plans at least 24 hours in advance of all planned teaching.
- Discussing each plan and offering suggestions prior to teaching; encouraging independent, creative thinking in planning, use of materials, motivation, and teaching approaches.
- Withholding criticism during a lesson except in instances where mistakes are made.

- Helping to develop consistent classroom management techniques that support learning, self-control, and respect for others.
- Encouraging a working environment in which you feel poised and confident.
- Modeling ways to address individual differences so that the students in the classroom develop a sense of affiliation, security and achievement.
- Supporting the habit of constant self-assessment, including post-lesson analyses.
- Encouraging and supporting rapport between you and the classroom students; cultivating a collegial, professional working relationship.

Conferencing

- Regularly held conferences promote your successful development during the student teaching practicum.
- Conferences may involve two or more individuals (e.g., mentor teacher, student teacher, university supervisor, building administrator).
- Conferences can be scheduled or can be spontaneous; they can be formal or informal.
- Each participant should understand the purpose of the conference and should feel free to play an active role in contributing, suggesting, and listening.

Assessment

- Weekly written observation feedback and/or updates are necessary for your continual growth throughout the experience.
- Letters of reference are to be written by both the mentor teacher and the university supervisor and are included with the final assessment. These letters go into your

credential file and are referenced by prospective employers.

- The following evaluation forms* will be completed in order to report your performance:

FORM:	*COMPLETED BY:*	*AT MIDT -ERM*	*AT FIN AL*
PSU Performance-Based Assessment (Form ST-1) w/accompanying narrative at final	*- University supervisor - Mentor teacher - Student teacher (optional at the direction of supervisor*	*YES YES YES*	*YES YES YES*

FORM:	*COMPLET-ED BY:*	*AT MIDT-ERM:*	*AT FINAL:*
PDE 430	*- University Supervisor ONLY*	*YES*	*YES*
Midterm Goals Sheet	*- Student Teacher*	*YES*	*NO*
PSU Discipline Specific Form (SEC ED & WL only)	*- University Supervisor - Mentor teacher*	*NO NO*	*YES YES*

*Information regarding assessment forms and guidelines for their use are found in Appendices B-H.

1.6 The Role of the Principal and Other School Personnel

The principal or building administrator either places you in the school or delegates this responsibility. The principal and other school personnel may orient you to the school culture in various ways, including some of the following:

- Making introductions to relevant faculty and staff.
- Discussing school policies, rules, regulations, and general procedures, including use of school resources, attendance at school district in-service, lunch and transportation procedures, etc.
- Sharing a brief history and description of the school.
- Providing an orientation to the physical layout of the school.
- Providing information on the school calendar, including holidays, half-days, parent conference dates and faculty meetings.
- Establishing a place for receiving mail and school announcements.
- Acquainting you with the role of school administration as it applies to teachers, students, parents, school board and community.
- Meeting occasionally to determine how the student teaching experience is progressing. The principal or department chair may wish to observe you.
- Inviting participation in school functions.

1.7 Policies and Procedures

In order to ensure an optimal student teaching experience and to be in compliance with state and national accreditation expectations, the following policies and procedures guide Penn State student teaching:

1.7.1 Courses and Deferred Grades

Student teaching is a full-time activity with all stakeholders holding the expectation that this practicum take precedence for the duration of the student teaching semester. Additional course registrations other than those designated for the student teaching practicum and accompanying seminar will not be permitted. This policy rules out concurrent enrollment in courses described as correspondence, independent learning, distance education, online, continuing education, evening, weekend, and other resident credit courses taken at Penn State or other institutions.

Exceptions to this policy due to truly extenuating circumstances are extremely rare and will be made only upon consensus of relevant faculty and school district personnel. Petitions for exceptions must begin with your academic advisor. Deferred grades must be completed before the start of the student teaching semester. Students enrolled in an Independent Learning course must complete all lessons prior to the beginning of the student teaching practicum.

1.7.2 Code of Professional Practice and Conduct for Educators

Professional educators in the Commonwealth of Pennsylvania believe that the quality of their services directly influences the nation and its citizens. Professional educators recognize their primary responsibility to the student and the development of the student's potential. Central to that development is the professional educator's valuing the worth and dignity of every person, student and colleague alike; devotion to excellence; development of knowledge; and democratic principles.

To those ends, you will engage in continuing inquiry to best serve the interests and needs of students. Professional practices are behaviors and attitudes that are based on a set of values that the professional education community believes and accepts. These values are evidenced by your conduct toward students, colleagues, mentor teacher, university supervisor, and others in the education community.

As you become a professional educator, you will be expected to abide by this code. Pennsylvania's Code of Professional Practice and Conduct for Educators can be found at 22 Pa. Code §§ 235.1 - 235.11 Violation of the Code may constitute basis for reprimand and/or removal from the student teaching practicum.

Code of Conduct (Source PDE Website)

Section 1. Mission

The Professional Standards and Practices Commission is committed to providing leadership for improving the quality of education in this Commonwealth by establishing high standards for preparation, certification, practice and ethical conduct in the teaching profession.

Section 2. Introduction

(a) Professional conduct defines interactions between the individual educator and students, the employing agencies and other professionals. Generally, the responsibility for professional conduct rests with the individual professional educator. However, in this Commonwealth, a Code of Professional Practice and Conduct (Code) for certificated educators is required by statute and violation of specified sections of the Code may constitute a basis for public or private reprimand.

Violations of the Code may also be used as supporting evidence, though may not constitute an independent basis, for the suspension or revocation of a certificate. The Professional Standards and Practices Commission (PSPC) was charged by the act of December 12, 1973 (P. L. 397, No. 141) (24 P. S. § §

12-1251 - 12-1268), known as the Teacher Certification Law, with adopting a Code by July 1, 1991. See 24 P. S. § 12-1255(a)(10).

(b) This chapter makes explicit the values of the education profession. When individuals become educators in this Commonwealth, they make a moral commitment to uphold these values.

Section 3. Purpose

(a) Professional educators in this Commonwealth believe that the quality of their services directly influences the Nation and its citizens. Professional educators recognize their obligation to provide services and to conduct themselves in a manner which places the highest esteem on human rights and dignity. Professional educators seek to ensure that every student receives the highest quality of service and that every professional maintains a high level of competence from entry through ongoing professional development. Professional educators are responsible for the development of sound educational policy and obligated to implement that policy and its programs to the public.

(b) Professional educators recognize their primary responsibility to the student and the development of the student's potential. Central to that development is the professional educator's valuing the worth and dignity of every person, student and colleague alike; the pursuit of truth; devotion to excellence; acquisition of knowledge; and democratic principles. To those ends, the educator engages in continuing professional development and keeps current with research and technology.

Educators encourage and support the use of resources that best serve the interests and needs of students. Within the context of professional excellence, the educator and student together explore the challenge and the dignity of the human experience.

Section 4. Practices

(a) Professional practices are behaviors and attitudes that are based on a set of values that professional education community believes and accepts. These values are evidenced by the professional educator's conduct toward students and colleagues, and the educator's employer and community. When teacher candidates become professional educators in this Commonwealth, they are expected to abide by this section.

(b) Professional educators are expected to abide by the following:

1. Professional educators shall abide by the Public School Code of 1949 (24 P. S. § § 1-101 - 27-2702), other school laws of the Commonwealth, sections 1201(a)(1), (2) and (4) and (b)(1), (2) and (4) of the Public Employe Relations Act (43 P. S. § § 1101.1201(a)(1), (2) and (4) and (b)(1), (2) and (4)) and this chapter.
2. Professional educators shall be prepared, and legally certified, in their areas of assignment. Educators may not be assigned or willingly accept assignments they are not certified to fulfill. Educators may be assigned to or accept assignments outside their certification area on a temporary, short-term, emergency basis. Examples: a teacher certified in English filling in a class period for a physical education teacher who has that day become ill; a substitute teacher certified in elementary education employed as a librarian for several days until the district can locate and employ a permanent substitute teacher certified in library science.
3. Professional educators shall maintain high levels of competence throughout their careers.
4. Professional educators shall exhibit consistent and equitable treatment of students, fellow educators and parents. They shall respect the civil rights of all and

not discriminate on the basis of race, national or ethnic origin, culture, religion, sex or sexual orientation, marital status, age, political beliefs, socioeconomic status, disabling condition or vocational interest. This list of bases or discrimination is not all-inclusive.

5. Professional educators shall accept the value of diversity in educational practice. Diversity requires educators to have a range of methodologies and to request the necessary tools for effective teaching and learning.

6. Professional educators shall impart to their students principles of good citizenship and societal responsibility.

7. Professional educators shall exhibit acceptable and professional language and communication skills. Their verbal and written communications with parents, students and staff shall reflect sensitivity to the fundamental human rights of dignity, privacy and respect.

8. Professional educators shall be open-minded, knowledgeable and use appropriate judgment and communication skills when responding to an issue within the educational environment.

9. Professional educators shall keep in confidence information obtained in confidence in the course of professional service unless required to be disclosed by law or by clear and compelling professional necessity as determined by the professional educator.

10. Professional educators shall exert reasonable effort to protect the student from conditions which interfere with learning or are harmful to the student's health and safety.

Section 5. Conduct

Individual professional conduct reflects upon the practices, values, integrity and reputation of the profession. Violation of § § 235.6-235.11 may constitute an independent basis for private or public reprimand, and may be used as supporting evidence in cases of certification suspension and revocation.

Section 6. Legal obligations

(a)The professional educator may not engage in conduct prohibited by the act of December 12, 1973 (P. L. 397, No. 141) (24 P. S. § § 12-1251-12-1268), known as the Teacher Certification Law.

(b)The professional educator may not engage in conduct prohibited by:

1. The Public School Code of 1949 (24 P. S. § § 1-101-27-2702) and other laws relating to the schools or the education of children.
2. The applicable laws of the Commonwealth establishing ethics of public officials and public employes, including the act of October 4, 1978 (P. L. 883, No. 170) (65 P. S. § § 401-413), known as the Public Official and Employee Ethics Law.

(c) Violation of subsection (b) shall have been found to exist by an agency of proper jurisdiction to be considered an independent basis for discipline.

Section 7. Certification

The professional educator may not:

1. Accept employment, when not properly certificated, in a position for which certification is required.
2. Assist entry into or continuance in the education profession of an unqualified person.

3. Employ, or recommend for employment, a person who is not certificated appropriately for the position.

Section 8. Civil Rights

The professional educator may not:

1. Discriminate on the basis of race, National or ethnic origin, culture, religion, sex or sexual orientation, marital status, age, political beliefs, socioeconomic status; disabling condition or vocational interest against a student or fellow professional. This list of bases of discrimination is not all-inclusive. This discrimination shall be found to exist by an agency of proper jurisdiction to be considered an independent basis for discipline.
2. Interfere with a student's or colleague's exercise of political and civil rights and responsibilities.

Section 9. Improper personal or financial gain

1. Accept gratuities, gifts or favors that might impair or appear to impair professional judgment.
2. Exploit a professional relationship for personal gain or advantage.

Section 10. Relationships with students

The professional educator may not:

1. Knowingly and intentionally distort or misrepresent evaluations of students.
2. Knowingly and intentionally misrepresent subject matter or curriculum.
3. Sexually harass or engage in sexual relationships with students.
4. Knowingly and intentionally withhold evidence from the proper authorities about violations of the legal obligations as defined within this section.

Section 11. Professional relationships

The professional educator may not:

1. Knowingly and intentionally deny or impede a colleague in the exercise or enjoyment of a professional right or privilege in being an educator.
2. Knowingly and intentionally distort evaluations of colleagues.
3. Sexually harass a fellow employe.
4. Use coercive means or promise special treatment to influence professional decisions of colleagues.
5. Threaten, coerce or discriminate against a colleague who in good faith reports or discloses to a governing agency actual or suspected violations of law, agency regulations or standards.

The Code of Professional Practice and Conduct for Educators can be found at 22 Pa. Code §§235.1 - 235.11. All questions should be directed to the Professional Standards and Practices Commission at (717) 787-6576.

1.7.3 Guest-Host Relationship

Acceptance of an invitation to teach within a particular school creates a guest-host relationship. It is important to note that a "host" school district and classroom teacher accept a student teacher as a "guest" who is learning to teach. your acceptance of a placement assignment is predicated on the following understand about the Guest/Host relation ship.

- That you are expected to act in a professional manner at all times;

- That you need to abide by the regulations, procedures, instructional practices, living up to professional and personal expectations of the particular district to which you have been assigned; and
- That, if personal or professional behavior or ability to work as an effective prospective teacher in the learning environment is not compatible with the expectations of the school district, you may be asked to leave by either the University or the host school district.

In addition, the guest-host relationship requires proof of the following documents that protect your welfare as well as that of members of the school community:

- FBI Clearance
- Guest-Host Relationship Form
- Act 34 Criminal History Clearance
- Act 151 Child Abuse History Clearance
- Tuberculosis Test Report
- Professional Liability Insurance

Information about these forms and clearances is available online at: http://www.ed.psu.edu/educ/cife .

1.7.4 School/Community Norms

The prevailing norms for public school personnel sometimes conflict with the current life styles of University students. Be aware that your opinions may differ from the host school and/or community value system. Differences of opinion may range from trivia to relevant social issues—including music preference, hairstyles, clothing trends, civil rights, morality, government, topics of discussion and teacher-student relationships. When in doubt about what the community norms are, please ask your mentor teacher. It is your responsibility to graciously adjust to the school culture. Your signature on the Guest/Host form signifies this acceptance.

You will be held accountable for a certain standard of care regarding the welfare of your students. The expected standard of care for teachers of school-age children is influenced by several factors including student age, compulsory attendance and the power differential between teacher and student. What might be considered appropriate for the professor in a university classroom might not be appropriate for the teacher in a K-12 classroom.

Considering the following questions will be helpful in reaching wise conclusions about a reasonable course of action when it is necessary for you to make a decision:

- Who should be involved and how?
- Who needs to be consulted for input?
- Who needs to approve?
- Who needs to be informed?
- Who is responsible for the outcome?

1.7.5 Academic Integrity

Penn State students are expected to act with civility and personal integrity; respect all others' dignity, rights and property; and help create and maintain an environment in which all can succeed through their own efforts. Penn State believes that an environment of academic integrity is requisite to respect for self and others and a civil community. This perspective on academic integrity also applies to the student teaching semester.

Academic integrity includes a commitment not to engage in or tolerate acts of falsification, misrepresentation, or deception of any type. Such acts of dishonesty may include cheating or copying, plagiarizing, submitting another person's work as one's own, using Internet sources without citation, fabricating field data or citations, "ghosting" (having another person complete work or assignments), tampering with the work of another student, facilitating other students' acts of academic dishonesty, etc.

Penn State students charged with a breach of academic integrity will receive due process and, if the charge is found valid, academic sanctions may range, depending on the severity of the offense, from F or no credit for the assignment to F for the course.

The University's statement on academic integrity is available at http://www.psu.edu/dept/oue/aappm/G-9.html.

1.7.6 Presentation of Self

Presentation of self, including physical appearance, helps establish a reputation and authority among students and colleagues. Creating and maintaining a professional demeanor should be a full-time goal while working in the school setting.

Physical appearance is a concern when it distracts from student learning. Concerns most frequently involve hairstyles, jewelry, tattoos, and piercings. Immodesty, casualness, grooming, and hygiene also could be causes of concern. When in doubt, you should check with the mentor teacher and university supervisor before wearing or doing something you might later regret.

1.7.7 Attendance and Participation Obligations

1.7.7.1 Calendar

The University Supervisor will specify the starting and ending dates of the student teaching experience. It is possible that these dates will not completely correspond to the Penn State fall or spring semester calendar. In addition to following the school district calendar, you are expected to follow the mentor teacher's daily schedule. You are not permitted to participate in any job actions such as strikes, walk-outs, or picketing.

1.7.7.2 Holiday and Vacations

The Penn State student teacher follows the calendar of the host school district, including holidays and vacations. You are not permitted to take vacation time during the student teaching practicum unless it is scheduled in the host school district calendar and approved by the university supervisor.

1.7.7.3 Absence/Tardiness

The practicum is a full-time obligation and is designed to meet the requirements of state and national accreditation agencies. You have responsibilities to the mentor teacher, the district's students and the university. Because of these responsibilities, fulltime, punctual attendance in the school placement is expected and required.

Although there are no "sick days" or "personal days" in student teaching, absences from the school placement may be excused for personal illness and/or death(s) in your immediate family. Documentation may be required. You must do the following if it is necessary for you to be absent:

1. You must telephone the mentor teacher as soon as an absence is imminent.
2. You must also notify the university supervisor as well as any additional personnel specified by the mentor teacher, university supervisor, or building principal as soon as possible.

Attendance at weekly seminar also is required. Absence is excused only for personal illness and/or death(s) in your immediate family. The university supervisor is to be notified in advance of any absence.

Unexcused absences or tardiness in school placement and/or weekly seminar will negatively affect your evaluation, particularly in the area of "Fulfilling Professional

Responsibilities." Excessive absences and/or tardiness will result in termination of the student teaching experience. If an extenuating circumstance should occur that would impact attendance, the university supervisor should be contacted immediately. The university supervisor will consult with the mentor teacher, building principal, and teacher education program staff at University Park about ramifications.

1.7.7.4 Substitute Teaching, Coaching, etc.

Penn State does not permit student teachers to act as paid substitute teachers while the mentor teacher is absent. You are permitted and encouraged to teach and assume leadership for a classroom when the mentor teacher is absent, as long as the school district has provided a paid employee as a teacher-in-charge.

You are encouraged to participate in coaching and extracurricular activities to the extent these duties do not interfere with the primary student teaching responsibilities and expectations. At no time during the official student teaching experience may you receive payment from the school for such duties.

1.7.8 Teacher – Student Interaction

1.7.8.1 Confidential and Privileged Information

You will be exposed to various sources of confidential and privileged information, including student records, school and classroom problems, and faculty and parent-teacher meetings. Public disclosure of confidential information is a violation of human dignity and rights. In most circumstances, it is considered a breach of professional ethics.

You should seek out the school's regulations and procedures about the handling of confidential information.

For example, parents and students have legal rights that help regulate the type and amount of testing, taping, and interviewing in which students may participate. Students identified with special needs, too, have specific legal rights. It is extremely important that all privileged information be treated with honor and respect.

1.7.8.2 Corporal Punishment

Penn State student teachers may not administer nor participate in the administration of corporal punishment at any time. Not only is it against Penn State's philosophy and regulations, corporal punishment is illegal in Pennsylvania.

1.7.8.3 Suspected Child Abuse

Student teachers are obligated to report suspected child abuse to the mentor teacher because it is the mentor teacher's responsibility to report such suspicions following district policy and procedures. You also should discuss suspicions of child abuse with the university supervisor. You, as a student teacher, should not address these kinds of problems by yourself.

1.7.8.4 Private Interactions

Penn State student teachers should always meet with students in a visible public location, even for one-on-one tutoring, conferencing, or interviewing. Special care must be taken to ensure that the mentor teacher is aware of all of your interactions with students. You may not transport students in your own vehicle or visit students at their homes or non-school locations. Likewise, you should not meet with parents at non-school locations or without your mentor teacher being present.

1.7.9 Grading

The ultimate responsibility for your grade for the practicum rests with the university supervisor. Student teaching is graded on a letter basis (e.g., A, A-, etc.), not pass/fail. The full range of grades, including pluses and minuses, is available to the university supervisor. The final grade is based on the supervisor's overall assessment of your performance in the classroom and on other tasks, assignments, and expectations associated with the student teaching practicum and seminar. The university supervisor consults with the mentor teacher concerning the final grade and may seek input on performance from you and other relevant school or university personnel in order to make an informed decision about the final grade.

Final grades less than "C" are considered unsatisfactory, and mean that you would need to repeat the student teaching semester in its entirety in order to be eligible for initial teacher certification. See Section 3.5 FINAL GRADE for specific criteria for the awarding of final grades.

1.7.10 Internet Personalities and Professionalism

Privacy and free speech rights permit you to maintain and submit information on the Internet, including postings on Facebook.com, and other similar websites; however, you must consider how the information you post may be interpreted and used by colleagues, parents, administrators and, above all, students. When you decide to post personal and private information on the web, you run the risk that the information will be used publicly, and its use may not be to your benefit.

Please Consider

- Administrators, parents, and mentors browse postings on sites like Facebook.com, forming first impressions and judging the moral character of pre-service and practicing teachers.

- You cannot control how others judge you, fairly or unfairly, but you can control the information from which others make judgments.
- Students look to their teachers to model appropriate behaviors and choices. Students may not be able to distinguish between adult choices and appropriate behaviors for children. Further, behaviors and choices that may seem appropriate in private contexts may be inappropriate in public and professional situations.

Professional Guidelines

- Maintain separate sites for professional and personal use.
- Do not share your username or personal web-addresses with students.
- If you do have personal web-space, like Facebook.com, arrange for it to be password protected and readable only by friends or chosen members.
- Do not permit anyone to post on your site without your approval.

If you know that a student has accessed your personal site, make it clear to the student that this is an inappropriate way to communicate with you.

Answering machine or cell phone messages

Please be sure that your answers and messages are professional. Your answering machine message or voice mail message may be your first introduction to your supervisor, mentor teacher or a potential employer.

Chapter 2

The Student Teaching Assignments

2.1 Overview of the Assignments

The assignments are designed with cognizance of your developmental needs and abilities, and aim to provide you with an opportunity to reflect upon your work and to promote your personal and professional development. The exact pattern of the experience and the timeline for completing specific tasks and assignments could vary slightly by regional cohort of student teachers. Your university supervisor will provide you with a syllabus that specifies the exact requirements of the experience and the timeline for completing tasks and assignments.

2.2 Orientation to the Placement

After the placement is secured and conveyed to you, it is important to get to know more about the community, district, school building, mentor teacher, and students. Building a strong relationship with the mentor teacher should be among the first of your goals. A positive first impression makes a difference! After receiving permission from the university supervisor, you should initiate communication with the mentor teacher by phoning or emailing the teacher at the school. If possible, you should visit the teacher at the school prior to the start of your student teaching.

In addition to building a relationship, initial contact with the mentor teacher is an important opportunity to gather and exchange some critical information. You are required to provide your mentor teacher with a copy of the Student Teaching Handbook. Some additional items to consider are:

- Exchanging of phone numbers, email addresses, and mailing addresses;
- Confirming the expected date, time, and location of the first day of student teaching;
- Becoming familiar with the mentor teacher's daily and weekly schedule;
- Discussing what courses, subjects, units, topics, etc., will likely be taught;
- Determining whether curriculum materials such as texts, software, district curriculum guides should be picked up prior to the start of student teaching;
- Asking for a copy of any school or classroom rules, guidelines for classroom management, and other policies, relevant to managing the learning-teaching environment;
- Other items as suggested by the university supervisor.

University supervisors often require student teachers to send a written communication, thanking the mentor teacher for his or her willingness to host a student teacher. A copy of the letter is to be sent to the university supervisor, as well.

2.3 Assignments

2.3.1 Student Teaching Files

There are many assignments, tasks, forms, and other paperwork associated with the student teaching experience. You are required to keep all of this paperwork organized and accessible. You, the mentor teacher, or the university supervisor may use the paperwork at many different points during the experience, especially during the conferences about performance and for preparation of the student teaching performance portfolio.

Therefore, it is essential for you to have an efficient organizational system. Some student teachers purchase and use a portable file box or large accordion folder for this purpose. Others find a three ring binder with labeled tabs to be sufficient. The university supervisor may require a specific type of filing system.

2.3.2 Inquiry into Community, School, and Classroom

The purpose of this beginning phase of student teaching is to help you to become familiar with the community, school, and classroom context. You will need to locate and review documentation and Internet resources about the community and school. Some good resources include local newspapers and the following websites:

- Pennsylvania Department of Education website: www.pde.state.pa.us/k12/site/default.asp
- Your school district's website
- Standard and Poor's School Evaluation Services site for Pennsylvania: www.ses.standardandpoors.com/
- Good Schools Pennsylvania website: www.goodschoolspa.org

In addition, data about the community and school can be

obtained by unobtrusive observations and brief, informal interviews with key community and/or school personnel. Although some of this information can be collected prior to the start of student teaching, much information can only be collected after the student teaching practicum has begun.

The "Orientation to The School" assignment, found in Appendix J., helps you to become acquainted with school personnel and operational procedures. The data collected will be useful in understanding the school and its resources, opportunities, and challenges.

A three-to-five page written summary/report following the outline below, accompanied by any relevant supporting materials, including "Orientation to The School" assignment, observations of other teachers, and shadowing a student should be completed by the date specified by your university supervisor.

The summary must include:

- Community and district-level information/factors (e.g., rural/suburban/urban, population demographics, dominant community business/influences, potential resources available for your teaching, etc.)
- School-level factors (e.g., academic environment, school philosophy, physical layout, school initiatives, strategic planning goals, involvement of parents, areas of promise and problems, etc.)
- Classroom-level factors and student characteristics (e.g., classroom layout, demographics, formally identified special needs such as learning or physical disability, informally identified needs such as shyness, accommodations described in IEPs, classroom learning environment academic and behavioral expectations, etc.).

2.3.3 Typical Day Observation: "Shadowing" a Student

You can experience the school day from the student's

perspective by following the schedule of a specific student or class throughout the day. It is important for you to become acquainted with a cross section of the school.

Data gathered during the shadowing and subsequent reflections will enhance your understanding of the school's culture. Your supervisor may ask you to submit a written report of your shadowing experience. This experience is especially valuable for secondary education majors to complete.

2.3.4 Observation of other Educators

Observations of other teachers in and out of the assigned grade level or subject area can provide useful insights. Sometimes student teachers placed in a middle school setting wonder what it is like to teach high school seniors. Student teachers who primarily teach high performing students might like to visit a classroom with predominantly lower performers. It also can be useful to observe other professionals in the school to gain insight into how the whole school functions. The guidance counselor's office, special education classrooms, ELL classrooms, and athletic facilities are just some of the places to find other educational professionals to observe.

Both the mentor teacher and university supervisor should approve all observations of other educators before the observation takes place. You may be asked to prepare a journal entry or a brief report based on observations of other educators. It is recommended that you complete most observations early in the semester before assuming a full-time teaching load. Observations of other educators should be requested and arranged in advance. Professional courtesies and protocol should be observed, which includes thanking the person who provides the observation setting and, as always, maintaining confidentiality regarding what may be seen and heard in these observations.

Early observations in the mentor teacher's classroom can help you in becoming familiar with the environment, learning students names and classroom procedures, practicing systematic observation, and building teacher inquiry skills. Observations are most productive when made with a stated purpose or focus. You are expected to define (with the guidance of the mentor teacher and/or university supervisor) specific aspects of the situation to be observed before beginning the observation.

Various approaches to observation are include in Appendix I. and can be adapted for observations of experienced teachers. Data should be taken during every observation, followed by an analysis appropriate for the observation's focus.

Remember: Your goal is to observe other teachers so that you may learn about teaching. Your purpose is not to evaluate other educators!

2.3.5 Weekly Schedule

Each week, you will submit a weekly teaching and activity schedule to your university supervisor, according to a specific format. The schedule should accurately reflect the general daily schedule and specify activities for which you are personally responsible. The schedule helps in the organization of your work and assists your supervisor in planning an efficient observation schedule.

2.3.6 Daily Lesson Plans

As a Penn State student teacher you are required to demonstrate the ability to effectively plan and implement learning activities and assessments in the classroom. Lesson plans assist in the identification of specific learning outcomes, materials, procedures, and assessment techniques to be ısed in planning effective lessons. Lesson planning is a ınental process composed of many decisions.

All teachers spend time thinking about a series of important instructional decisions before their lessons begin. The written plans are evidence that this thinking process has occurred. The written plans also provide a window into your thinking about teaching and learning and allow the mentor teacher and university supervisor to assist with your development in that area.

Experienced teachers plan lessons in many different ways and at many different times. Since lesson planning is a mental process, experienced teachers often do not produce formal written plans for the lessons they will teach. This does not mean that their lessons are not well planned, and many experienced teachers would admit that producing written plans does in fact improve their planning and, subsequently, their teaching. As experienced teachers, they understand the process of lesson planning thoroughly, and they are able to plan lessons in more informal ways.

Beginning teachers and prospective teachers, however, are still in the process of developing an understanding of lesson planning and learning about the multitude of factors that must be considered in planning high quality instruction. Therefore, Penn State expects all student teachers to engage in the mental process of planning. This thought process is made evident via formal written plans.

The development of the written lesson plan serves three purposes. First, it stimulates and strengthens the mental process of planning a lesson. Second, it provides concrete evidence that you have considered important decisions and factors in planning. This then fulfills the third purpose: the detailed planning makes your thought process explicit so that your mentor teacher and university supervisor can help you plan more effectively.

Written plans are required for all lessons and learning activities that you expect to implement. Your mentor teacher must approve your lesson plans at least 24 hours in advance of teaching. Advanced planning provides a point of discussion with your mentor teacher that can facilitate cooperative planning, clarification and trouble- shooting. If your written lesson plans are not submitted at least 24 hours in advance, the University recommends that you not be permitted to implement the lesson or learning activity. Please refer to the planning resources in the appendix.

2.3.7. Lesson Analysis

Because an analysis of lessons taught is critical to the development of teachers, you may be asked to prepare a written analysis of some or all of the lessons taught. As you reflect on the most and least effective aspects of the lesson and identify alternatives, you will develop abilities to inquire into your own practices that will foster continued professional growth and improvement. The analysis is conducted shortly after teaching a lesson. In an effort to analyze the effectiveness of the lesson, you should ask yourself the following questions:

- What did I learn through the process of planning and implementing this lesson?
- What did my students learn? How do I know what they learned?
- To what extent did I meet the needs of all of my learners? How do I know whether I have?
- What did I learn about teaching and learning concept?
- What did I learn about managing the learning environment during this lesson?
- What did I really like about this lesson?
- What disappointed me about this lesson?
- What alternative instructional and assessment strategies could I have used?
- What will I do next?

2.3.8 Emergency Lesson Plans

You are required to prepare emergency lesson plans to be used in unexpected situations such as schedule changes. The emergency plans should be readily available for immediate use. The plans are written and contain the same parts needed in all good planning, such as objectives, materials, procedures, assessment of self and students. Emergency lesson plans may be independent of other lessons and need not be an integral part of the curriculum.

The approximate length of emergency lesson plans should be varied (e.g., two or three plans to run between five and ten minutes; one plan for ten to twenty minutes; one for twenty to thirty minutes [or a class period]). All activities should be appropriate to the interest and grade level of the students.

You should be able to put an emergency plan into action smoothly and without hesitation. In fact, the emergency plan should be developed well enough that any teacher could put the plan into action. Therefore, all materials should be ready to use without additional preparation. Activities for an emergency plans may be challenging and thought-provoking (e.g., mind benders or mazes) and/or may be intended for one or more of the following:

- Relaxation
- Appreciation
- Recreation
- Developing creativity
- Reinforcement of a skill
- Reinforcement of facts needing later recall
- Enrichment
- Greater breadth of application and/or understanding in any knowledge area previously present.

2.3.9 Personal Philosophy

All student teachers bring beliefs about learning and teaching to the field experience. These beliefs might include the way children and teenagers grow and develop, the purposes of schooling, the nature of learning, teaching, educational programs, and school climate and structure. This platform of beliefs is often based on one's own experiences in schools and upon learning principles or theories studied.

At the beginning of the practicum, you will be asked to express your personal philosophy in writing. You likely prepared a philosophy statement in courses prior to student teaching—it would prove helpful to take it out and review it when planning for instruction and interaction with students. You may find inconsistencies due to the fact that teaching is a process of continual inquiry—changes and modifications in philosophy are considered healthy and necessary.

The student teaching practicum affords you with many opportunities to test your beliefs and to determine the extent to which your aims or goals are primary, rational, and applicable to practice. Activities to help clarify beliefs about teaching and learning can include:

- Observing experienced teachers to identify instances of effective teaching strategies and methods.
- Discussing and reflecting on these teaching strategies or methods with the mentor teacher to determine why these practices are used and to identify the underlying learning principles
- Using analysis/observations of classroom implementation and interaction by the supervisor and mentor teacher.

Near the end of the practicum, you should examine the philosophy that you wrote earlier in the semester and determine which beliefs prevailed and were reinforced and why. It will be helpful to your growth if you can determine which beliefs changed and why. You may be asked to write a revised philosophy of teaching and learning that is appropriate for a job interview.

2.3.10 Video Analysis

Analysis of a video or audio recording of a lesson taught provides you with an opportunity (a) to reflect more intensively on teaching and learning, and (b) to use systematic observation skills independently to assess teacher-learner behaviors. **You must be knowledgeable of any district policies regarding video recording prior to recording a lesson.**

Video recording is generally preferable to audio recording, unless the focus of the analysis is on vocal qualities (enunciation, volume, changes in inflection), dialect or accent, or on questioning skills. Viewing the video once without collecting data or taking notes enables you to see yourself in front of the group and listen to the variety of classroom sounds captured on video. In this way, the focus can be maintained during subsequent viewings.

A focus for analysis should first be identified. You can then view the video, collect relevant data from viewing the video, and prepare an analysis. The analysis should be a two-to-three page narrative with any appropriate attachments (e.g., copy of the lesson plan, copy of a data summary sheet, a complete analysis). The following components should be included in the written video analysis:

- Description of the area of focus and indication why this particular aspect of teaching was selected;
- Explanation of the rationale for the focus, and careful consideration of principles of learning and best practice;

- Collection and organization of data related to the focus from viewing the tape one or more times (e.g., chart of some other approach to systematic data organization);
- Summary of the findings and discussion of their meaning;
- Discussion of any unexpected discoveries that merit attention;
- Setting of specific goals for improvement and listing of at least two specific changes to be made that will help you to achieve identified goals.

Some areas for analysis might include:

- Questioning techniques (use of Bloom's Taxonomy; distribution of questions by gender, ability, interest, wait time);
- Response to students' answers (use of positive reinforcement statements; verbatim repetition, allowing students to elaborate on their answers or other students' answers, seeking a correct response if a student's answer is incomplete or inaccurate);
- Teacher clarity (in giving directions, explaining content through task analysis, making explanations relevant to the process or the product, pacing);
- Types and frequency of praise and encouragement. It is helpful for you and your mentor teacher to watch the video together.

2.3.11 Journal Writing

Keeping a journal during student teaching encourages reflection in a less structured format. Entries may include experiences, reactions, activities and learning related to the art of teaching. It may be a reflective document that brings together events, reactions, and response to the school day. It also may be a tool for communication with the supervisor.

Suggested topics for reflection in the journal include:

- Comparison of teaching and management strategies among observed teachers;
- Thoughts about topics as parent/teacher relations, faculty interaction, and student affairs;
- Discussion of classroom/behavior management strategies;
- Reflections on abilities to work with special needs students, or with small and large groups;
- Insights about attitudes toward teaching and educational concerns;
- Periodic self-assessments in the areas of professional growth and development including knowledge about children and teaching;
- Descriptions of peak experiences, crisis, surprising occurrences or other events which appear significant to professional growth;
- Reactions to current professional literature or research.

2.3.12 Peer Consultation/Observation

Observations of peers provide a different perspective on teaching and provide an opportunity to collaborate toward the goal of improving teaching skills, not to make critical judgments. Since most experienced teachers are observed infrequently, this experience may provide a foundation for collaborative observations and teaching experiences in the future. A useful strategy is the three-part observation cycle:

1. The pre-observation conference—to determine what the observer should look for and collect data about;
2. The actual observation; and
3. A post-observation conference—what the observer saw and what it means to be the teacher. Please see Appendix I for some suggested observation strategies.

2.3.13 Individual Project: Response to Intervention

This semester long teacher inquiry project requires you, in collaboration with other professionals, to identify an exceptional student, gather data, analyze the data, prescribe and implement adaptations, and evaluate the resultant effects. In addition to providing valuable assistance to an individual school student, this inquiry project aids in developing your sense of efficacy as a teacher.

With confidentiality always a priority, you will consult with other professionals such as learning support teachers, school psychologists, and school counselors. You will research the student's background and report on the student's current level, strengths, and weaknesses at the beginning of the semester. After doing background research, you will clearly define the targeted behavior, and gather baseline data on your student. You will then define instructional and/or behavioral goals for your student, and identify strategies to achieve these goals.

You will continue to gather data as you implement your plan of intervention. Throughout this project, you will reflect on the strategies that you use and analyze their effectiveness. If your initial intervention does not work, you are encouraged to try other intervention strategies. Your university supervisor will provide you with detailed guidelines appropriate for your specific classroom setting.

2.3.14 Unit Plan — Inquiry into Teaching: Planning, Teaching, and Reflecting

Once oriented to the community, school, and classroom, the focus shifts to greater collaboration with your mentor teacher for planning, teaching, and assessment. You will engage in activities ranging from assessing or tutoring individual students to working with small group to co-teaching the whole class. You also will participate in tasks such as preparing new instructional materials, grading, etc.

While there will be many opportunities to plan, teach, assess, and reflect during student teaching, Penn State student teachers must plan, teach, and assess the impact of a standard-based unit. In consultation with your university supervisor and mentor teacher, you will develop a unit of instruction and assessment that lasts for a recommended minimum length of 10 days, depending on the context. This core assignment has several major components:

Component #1: Inquiry into the Curriculum

The following sub-components should be clearly identifiable:

a. Identify Standards: Identify district and state academic standards that should be met by students upon completion of this unit of instruction. PA Academic Standards can be found at http://www.pde.state.pa.us/k12/site/default.asp (Click on "Academic Standards" along left column and follow the links to relevant subject area) as well as through the "Standards Wizard" on Taskstream. These standards provide a framework to help teachers identify teaching and learning priorities and are necessary in guiding the design of curriculum, instruction, and assessments. Another valuable source can be the Pennsylvania Department of Education's Standards Aligned System (SAS). Information about SAS can be found at the following URL: www.pdesas.org

b. Specify Learning Outcomes: In order to meet the specified district and state standard(s), what will the students need to know, understand and be able to do? Understanding is more than just textbook knowledge and basic skills. Understanding involves sophisticated insights of concepts and abilities. What concepts or "enduring understandings" should students develop by the end of the lesson sequence? In addition to the "big ideas," what key knowledge/facts and skills should students demonstrate to meet the learning outcomes of the unit?

c. Develop Assessment and Instruction Plan: Now that the end is clear, it is time to design the means for getting the students there. Using the standards and specific learning outcomes that were identified in (A) and (B) as the starting point, develop an integrated instruction and assessment plan of at least 10 lessons that builds on community and school context information and is aligned and keyed to the learning outcomes and standards specified above. At this point in the planning process, the instruction and assessment plan may take either of two forms:

1. A block plan that briefly states the specific learning outcomes, learning activities, formative assessment strategy, and key materials for each lesson; or
2. Fully developed lesson plans for each day using the lesson plan format agreed upon by you, your mentor, and the university supervisor. If the block plan format is used in planning the unit, fully developed lesson plans for each lesson will need to be developed at least 24 hours in advance. If the fully developed lesson plan format is used in planning the unit, the daily lessons will need to be revised as necessary to adapt to student learning and the actual progress of instruction during the course of the unit. The revisions to the lesson plans must be completed at least 24 hours in advance.

Note that it is expected that the instructional plan for the unit meaningfully integrates instructional technology as appropriate for the learning outcomes and for the school/classroom context. You must consult with the mentor while developing this plan to be sure it can be implemented in the assigned classroom. See various planning and assessment resources in Appendix L.

Assessment is the act of determining the extent to which curricular goals are met and achieved. How will the teacher know if students have developed the understandings specified? What will be accepted as evidence that students have developed the desired understandings? By planning assessments while planning instruction, the assessments can serve as teaching targets— helping to sharpen instructional plans to be sure they meet intended outcomes.

The assessment plan must include:

1. Pre-assessments (diagnostic) to help you understand what students already know and are able to do and/or "diagnose" learning needs;
2. Ongoing assessments (formative) that are used during the unit to monitor the development of understanding and provide data that help "to inform" you of the next instructive step;
3. Post-assessments (summative), which may consist of selected response items (e.g., multiple choice, matching), constructed response items (e.g., short answer, label diagram, concept map), assignment artifacts (e.g., essay, drawing, journal entry), or performances (e.g., oral presentations, debate). In addition, informal assessments such as observations or clinical assessments such as an interview, think- aloud, or "science talk" are also suitable forms of post-instructional assessment. Post-assessments "summarize" student learning.

(d) Plan Accommodations. In addition to external standards and local school district expectations, you also should consider the specific needs of students when designing learning and assessment experiences. Therefore, you are required to:

1. Identify the students (use pseudonym) with identified special needs (if there are no identified students in the classroom, your mentor teacher could assist in selecting

a student who can be considered exceptional for some reason).

2. Describe a minimum of one adaptation or accommodation for those students for each lesson in the unit.
3. Clearly identify this adaptation in each lesson plan

(e) Plan the Learning Environment. What plans have been developed for a safe and supportive learning environment where learners can achieve the outcomes specified in the instructional plan? You must demonstrate that consideration has been given to creating an inviting and motivating atmosphere, how to implement procedures to effectively manage class time and resources, and how to respond to potential student misbehavior. The plan for the learning environment should be embedded into each daily lesson plan.

Component # 2: Teach the Unit

Once the unit is planned and approved by your mentor teacher and university supervisor, you need to gather necessary materials and supplies and begin teaching. While teaching the unit, arrangements should be made to be formally observed at least once by your university supervisor and once by your mentor teacher. Formal observations will provide useful information that can facilitate improvement as a teacher. In some cases, the supervisor or mentor may expect that at least one lesson is videotaped for self-analysis and/or that a journal be kept wherein you reflect on each lesson taught. In addition, use of observational data in Component #4 permits an assessment of your own teaching during this unit.

Component #3 Inquiry into Student Learning

This inquiry requires you to analyze and use student assessment data to characterize what has been learned during the unit. There are two parts to this inquiry.

Whole Class Assessment: The purpose is to organize and analyze assessment evidence in order to draw conclusions about student achievement of each of the specified learning outcomes. The best way to conduct this kind of assessment is to examine and compare pre-instructional assessments and post-instructional assessments targeting the same concept of understanding. It is not necessary to report analyses for each individual child.

Rather, you should aggregate assessment information of the whole class to show what students learned and are now able to do. What patterns of performance are evident in the assessments? Are these the results expected? In what areas did the students perform best and worst? What misconceptions, if any, are revealed by the assessments?

Individual Student Assessment: In this sub-component, the task is to organize and analyze assessment evidence for at least one student identified with special needs, exceptionality, etc. The purpose is to demonstrate your ability to monitor and interpret the academic performance of an exceptional child and reflect on your own ability to differentiate instruction. What patterns of performance are evident in the assessment? Are these the results expected? In what areas did the student (or students) perform best and worst? What misconceptions, if any, are revealed by the assessments?

Component #4 Inquiry into My Teaching

The purpose of Component #4 is to scaffold your reflection on your own development as a new teacher. There are three parts to this inquiry.

Overall Self-Assessment: Provide an overall assessment of teaching strengths and limitations during this unit of instruction. The "Teacher Education Performance

Standards" (see Appendix A) in the areas of Planning and Preparing for Student Learning, Teaching, Analyzing Student Learning and Inquiring into Teaching, and Fulfilling Professional Responsibilities are used to guide the reflection process. You are to indicate at least one strength and one limitation for each of the four performance domains.

Examples from lesson plans, formal observations, videotapes, student assessment data, peer observation notes, etc., can be used to illustrate each strength and limitation in each of these performance areas.

Perception of Effectiveness with Exceptional Student: You are required to assess the effectiveness of adaptations and accommodations made for an exceptional learner and provide reflections on the effectiveness of the instructional differentiation and resource adaptations utilized. Examples from lesson plans, formal observations, videotapes, student assessment data, peer observation notes, lesson analyses/ reflections, etc. can be used to illustrate the assessment.

Goal Setting: Student teaching is not the end; it is just the beginning of a rewarding career as a caring, effective educator. An appropriate conclusion to this inquiry into one's teaching is to set achievable goals in each of the four performance domains for future growth and development.

2.3.15 Required Assignments for Short Term Student Teaching Abroad

A. Assignments to be completed in U.S. Placement

1. Inquiry into Teaching and Learning Project
    a. Inquiry into School and Community
    b. Inquiry into Curriculum
    c. Inquiry into Teaching and Learning
    d. Individual Learner Project

2. Mid-semester Performance Framework Portfolio

B. Assignments to be completed in International Placement

1. Final Performance Framework Portfolio
2. Weekly journal entries submitted via email to U.S. Supervisor

a. Suggested topics

(i) Orientation to international school and community

(ii) Comparison between PA school and host nation school (facilities, dress, student-teacher relationships, classroom management, assessment, etc.)

(iii) Reflections on accommodations for individual learners in the host nation school

(iv) Self-assessment of teaching, especially in reference to goals developed in PA placement

(v) Student/youth culture in the host nation (secondary) or views of childhood/children in host nation (elementary)

(vi) Cultural views on education in host nation (parental involvement, government support, private vs. public schools, etc.)

(vii)Reflection on the entire semester (How have you grown and changed? What have you learned?)

Chapter 3

Assessment of the Student Teacher

3.1 OVERVIEW

The student teaching experience is a culmination of years of preparation. Yet, at the same time, it is just a beginning. You, as a student teacher, are not expected to be a master teacher. You are at the very early stage of a teaching career and are just beginning to formulate understandings and practices that help all students learn. Consequently, the student teaching assessment and evaluation processes have been designed to support your reflection and growth while simultaneously providing evidence about your accomplishments.

The Penn State Teacher Education Performance Framework (see Appendix A) describes your expected performances in four major domains of practice:

- Planning and Preparing for Student Learning
- Teaching
- Analyzing Student Learning and Inquiring into Teaching

- Fulfilling Professional Responsibilities

Each domain identifies critical understandings, abilities, and dispositions that you, as a Penn State teacher candidate, should know, understand, be able to do, and exemplify in your work as a teacher.

During the student teaching semester, there will be many opportunities for you to conference with your mentor teacher and university supervisor about your performance as a new professional. Formative assessments will clarify where you are at a given point and where you need to go in terms of professional growth. You will be provided with verbal and written feedback throughout the practicum.

This section of the Penn State Student Teaching Handbook will focus on the student teaching performance portfolio and two important parts of the assessment process - the mid-semester evaluation and the final evaluation. The portfolio, mid-semester, and final assessment processes contribute to the your overall assessment, as required by Chapter 49 of the Pennsylvania School Code, in the areas of basic skills and general knowledge, professional knowledge and practice, and subject matter knowledge.

3.2 Student Teaching Performance Portfolio

The Student Teaching Performance Portfolio is a purposeful and organized selection of evidence that demonstrates how you have accomplished the performance expectations set forth in the Penn State Teacher Education Performance Framework (see Appendix A). The portfolio is different from the filing system being maintained, in that the filing system contains all paperwork and related items for the whole semester. The Student Teaching Performance Portfolio contains works that you carefully select and extract from the files in order to demonstrate what you have accomplished as a student teacher. The Student Teaching Performance Portfolio is the natural complement to the Penn State Performance-Based Assessment of Student Teaching form; it is the place to assemble and reflect on evidence used to derive ratings of performance.

The portfolio allows you to:

- Experience a professional portfolio process such as the one used in statewide beginning teacher programs in several states and used by experienced teachers seeking National Board for Professional Teaching Standards Certification.
- Provide specific examples of work related to all performance standards to your mentor teacher and university supervisor for discussion and reflection throughout the experience, especially during the performance assessment conferences.
- Have an organized collection of evidence of performance to use during job interviews.
- Share evidence of accomplishments with Penn State faculty so they can assess the quality of the teacher preparation program.

Organize your portfolio around each of the performance domains in the *Penn State Teacher Educational Performance Framework*. The level of performance achieved in *each standard* should be addressed by referencing at least two artifacts contained in the portfolio, **with reference to at least one piece required at mid-semester to make a compelling argument of performance to that point in time.**

A significant value of the portfolio lies in your reflection about the process of selecting the artifacts you use as evidence to be included in the portfolio. A written justification will accompany each piece of evidence. Simply put, these justifications provide the rationale for its inclusion. Portfolios are most useful when they support your personal *process* of learning to teach, rather than merely the *products* of your learning.

3.3 Penn State Performance-based Assessment (See Appendices B & C)

3.3.1 Mid-Semester Assignment

The midterm conference is a time for a formal, data-based discussion about your progress. The discussion takes place with you, your mentor teacher, and your university supervisor. The mid-semester conference is facilitated by your university supervisor and generally follows this pattern:

1. You, your mentor teacher, and your university supervisor complete the Penn State Performance-Based Assessment of Student Teaching (Form ST-1). The ST-1 form can be found at www.ed.psu.edu/educ/cife. The supervisor will specify whether each person should complete the form independently or together as a group. In either case, each person should attempt to indicate an honest appraisal of performance in each of the major domains of practice listed on the form. Ratings should be made relative to (1) the indicators on the assessment form and (2) evidence from the first half of the student teaching experience. In addition, the Pennsylvania Statewide Evaluation Form (PDE 430) required by the Pennsylvania Department of Education, will be completed by the university supervisor only. See information regarding all assessment forms in the Appendices B-E, and G.
2. You, your mentor teacher, and your university supervisor meet at the mid-semester conference to review and discuss current performance. The conference

also is used to set goals for the remainder of the experience.

3. Based on this mid-semester conference, your supervisor will prepare verbal and written summaries of the ratings in each performance area and of the expectations and goals for the remainder of the semester. You will complete the form entitled, "Mid-semester Goals and Strategies for the Second Half of the Semester." See Appendix F.

NOTE: The mid-semester conference may result in a determination that you are not making adequate progress based on the expectations stated for student teaching in this Handbook. If your supervisor determines that an overall satisfactory rating will not be possible by the end of the experience, you will be referred to either the Elementary or the Secondary Coordinator of Curriculum & Instruction Field Experiences, who will determine the next steps.

3.3.2 Final Assessment

The process for conducting the final assessment is similar to the process for conducting the mid-semester assessment. You, your mentor teacher, and your university supervisor complete the Penn State Performance- Based Assessment of Student Teaching. Once again, a three-way conference is held to review performance and discuss ratings on the assessment form and determine if Mid-semester Goals and Strategies have been met for the second half of the semester.

Although it is desirable that consensus between your mentor teacher and university supervisor be reached concerning the grade to be issued, the final decision and subsequent reporting of the grade is the responsibility of your university supervisor. After the conference, the university supervisor forwards all necessary documentation of your performance to the Field Experience Office. An electronic copy of The Penn State Performance-Based

Assessment of Student Teaching will be forwarded to the Penn State Career Services Office for inclusion in the e-credentials file for employment purposes. This is your only access to this assessment that includes references from your university supervisor and mentor teacher.

It is your responsibility to activate the e-credentials file by contacting the Career Services Office (814-865-2377) in 101 Bank of America Building, Career Services Center, and University Park, PA 16802 (http://www.sa.psu.edu/career/).

3.4 Pennsylvania Statewide Evaluation Form (See Appendices D & E)

The Pennsylvania Statewide Evaluation Form for Student Professional Knowledge and Practice (PDE 430), as previously noted, is mandated by the Pennsylvania State Legislature and must be administered by all Pennsylvania institutions offering teacher certification programs. The assessment form will be utilized twice—at mid-semester and at the end of the semester (final) and is completed by the University Supervisor only. You can access this form at http://www.teaching.state.pa.us/teaching/cwp/view.asp?a=90&pm=1&Q=32539

3.5 Final Grade

A final grade will denote the University Supervisor's professional judgment of the quality of your overall performance during your student teaching semester. Your university supervisor, in consultation with your mentor teacher, will assess your performance in the classroom. Overall performance, however, includes participation and accomplishment in non-classroom components as well, such as the student teaching seminar. The grade, therefore, will be based upon all aspects of your performance. This includes the quality of (1) achievement of the standards specific to the individual's certification program and (2) other practicum and seminar requirements. The grade will reflect both the level of performance and the amount of support needed as a beginning teacher. A letter grade of A, A-, B+, B, B-, C+, C, D or F will be assigned.

Criteria for an "A" Grade: A student teacher may be awarded an "A" grade when it can be stated unequivocally that she or he is fully capable of beginning the first years of teaching demonstrating true excellence. The student teacher must have met all the provisions of the "B" grade in an exceptional manner and demonstrated a high degree of effectiveness in working cooperatively with peers and other educational professionals in the setting of the student teaching assignment. He or she will have demonstrated exceptional achievement in attaining competency as judged by qualified professionals charged with supervision and will require minimal support as a beginning teacher.

Criteria for a "B" Grade: A "B" grade in student teaching is indicative of moderate achievement in student teaching as judged by qualified professionals charged with the supervision of student teachers. It is above the level of minimally acceptable achievement. The student teacher may require some support at the beginning of the first teaching assignment as is common for beginning teachers.

Criteria for a "C" Grade: A "C" in student teaching means that the student teacher has demonstrated minimally acceptable achievement. All competencies must have been achieved. A "C" grade indicates that she or he will need considerable support when entering the teaching profession. Performance below a "C" level, because of its impact on school children in the field setting, is not acceptable for certification and could result in dismissal from the practicum.

Chapter 4

Appendix A

Penn State Teacher Education Performance Framework

Domain A: Planning and Preparing for Student Learning. The Penn State teacher plans instruction and assessments based upon robust knowledge of subject matter, students and their learning and development, curriculum goals and standards, and the community.

A1. The teacher demonstrates an understanding of subject matter and subject-specific pedagogy during planning.

A2. The teacher uses principles of learning and development, and understanding of learners and learner diversity during planning of instruction and assessment.

A3. The teacher uses relevant community, district, school, and classroom factors and characteristics in planning.

A4. The teacher develops and selects appropriate instructional goals and objectives.

A5. The teacher designs coherent short range and long range opportunities for student learning and assessment.

A6. The teacher selects, adapts, and/or creates appropriate instructional resources and materials, including instructional technologies.

A7. The teacher plans for an inclusive, nurturing, stimulating, and academically challenging learning environment.

Domain B: Teaching. The Penn State teacher actively encourages students' development and learning by creating a positive classroom learning environment, appropriately using a variety of instructional and assessment strategies and resources, including instructional technologies.

B1. The teacher actively and effectively engages all learners

B2. The teacher assesses student learning in multiple ways in order to monitor student learning, assist students in understanding their progress, and report student progress.

B3. The teacher appropriately manages classroom procedures.

B4. The teacher appropriately manages student learning and behavior.

B5. The teacher communicates effectively using verbal, nonverbal, and media communication techniques while teaching.

Domain C: Analyzing Student Learning and Inquiring into Teaching. The Penn State teacher continually and systematically inquires into the quality of his or her teaching and the conditions of schooling in order to enhance student learning and development.

C1. The teacher monitors and adjusts instructional and assessment strategies during teaching.

C2. The teacher systematically analyzes assessment data to characterize performance of whole class and relevant sub-groups of students.

C3. The teacher uses data from his/her own classroom teaching to evaluate his/her own strengths and areas for improvement.

Domain D: Fulfilling Professional Responsibilities. The Penn State teacher exhibits the highest standards of professionalism in all that he/she does.

D1. The teacher consistently meets expectations and fulfills responsibilities.

D2. The teacher establishes and maintains productive, collaborative relationships with colleagues and families.

D3. The teacher values and seeks professional growth.

D4. The teacher continuously demonstrates integrity, ethical behaviors, and appropriate professional conduct.

APPENDIX B.

Guidelines for Using the Penn State Performance-Based Assessment of Student Teaching

The Performance-Based Assessment of Student Teaching focuses on performances within four major domains included in the Penn State Model of Teacher Preparation:

a. Planning and Preparing for Student Learning

b. Teaching

c. Analyzing Student Learning and Inquiring into Teaching

d. Fulfilling Professional Responsibilities.

Each domain identifies critical understandings, abilities, and dispositions that Penn State teacher candidates should know and be able to do in their work as teachers. The mid-term and end-of-term assessment process contributes to a candidate's overall assessment, as specified in Chapter 49 of the Pennsylvania School Code, in the areas of basic skills and general knowledge, professional knowledge and practice, and subject matter knowledge.

There are three kinds of assessments reported on this assessment form. First, the student is assessed on a specific Standard in a specific Domain of performance, e.g. Standard A1. Secondly, the student is given an overall Domain Assessment, e.g. Domain A - Planning and Preparing for Student Learning. Domain assessments report candidate performance across several related Standards in a single performance Domain. Finally, an Overall Rating reports the assessor's professional judgment of the candidate's overall achievement and reflects the student's readiness to assume a teaching position.

For each of the Standards, there are ratings of "Consistently," "Often," "Sometimes," "Rarely" and "Not Observed." "Consistently" is used when the performance always or almost always matches or exceeds the description. "Often" is used when the performance matches or exceeds the description most of the time but falls below now and then. "Sometimes" is used when the performance on this standard matches or exceeds the description about half or a little more than half of the time. "Rarely" is used when the performance fails to match or exceed the description more than half the time. "Not Observed" indicates that performance on this standard has not yet been observed.

For each of the Domain ratings, the following description are used:

Exemplary: The candidate is highly sophisticated and insightful, unusually thorough and consistent in ability to draw on extensive knowledge of learners and teaching to create and adjust powerful learning opportunities. Is highly aware of strengths and limitations; actively pursues professional growth. The candidate has earned a "Consistently" for all or nearly all Standard indicators.

Good: The candidate's performance is of moderately high quality. In nearly all circumstances the candidate is able to adequately draw on knowledge of learners and learner discovery to create appropriate learning opportunities. The candidate can articulate strengths and limitations as well as plan for continued professional growth. The candidate has earned a typical rating of "Often" with some ratings of "Consistently."

Satisfactory: The candidate is performing at the minimum level expected of a new teacher. The candidate has basic but appropriate understandings of learning and teaching. Ability to be adaptive, creative, and innovative is limited. Appears to be somewhat aware of limitations. May require close supervision and support as a new teacher in order to become proficient. The candidate has earned typical ratings of "Often" or "Sometimes."

Needs Improvement: Candidate has shown limited progress but needs significant improvement. The candidate's performance typically fails to meet expectations in one or two areas. Typical ratings are "sometimes" with one or two ratings of "rarely."

Unsatisfactory: The candidate relies on a limited repertoire of routines, can perform only with coaching, relies on highly scripted procedures or approaches, and is generally unaware of limitations. The candidate is not prepared to be a first-year teacher. The candidate earned a rating of "rarely" in two or three areas or with a rating so significantly deficient in one or more areas that the overall performance on this Domain is unsatisfactory.

For the "OVERALL RATING," the same descriptors are used, but the rating of "Needs Improvement" is no longer used. For information about the process for determining the appropriate letter grade for the experience, please refer to Section 3.5 in the Handbook.

Mid-semester Assessment

- Student teachers, mentor teachers, and university supervisors complete the PSU Performance-Based Assessment Form, indicating strengths and areas needing improvement.
- Mid-semester Goals and Strategies Sheet is completed with input from student teacher, mentor teacher, and university supervisor

Final Assessment

- Student teachers, mentor teachers, and university supervisors complete the PSU Performance-Based Assessment Form again, indicating strengths and areas needing improvement
- The narrative emphasizes the specific context and strengths and areas of growth for a particular student teacher. The narrative is considered by some to be as important as the assessment form.
- Students should receive a copy of the completed form, including narratives. Students should keep copies because PSU files are purged periodically—typically after five years.

APPENDIX C.

Pennsylvania State University
College of Education
Performance-based Assessment of Student Teaching
Revised 12/18/07

Candidate: (Last)_______(First)______ (Maiden MI)____

Student Identification #:________Certification Area:_______

Permanent Address (Street)______________________________

(City)______________ , (State)___________(Zip)__________

Student Teaching Experience: (circle one) Spring or Fall Semester, 20_____________Practicum Dates:__________

School District:____

School Building:____

City:______________________State:______________________

Grade Level (s):____

Mentor Teacher:____

Signature___________________________________

Date:____

Effective April 2005, Penn State Career Services established an electronic credentials service, eCredentials. Documents are now stored electronically and may be uploaded by reference writers, candidates, or Career Services staff who have authenticated their identities with a valid Penn State digital identity. This authentication serves as an electronic signature for those documents without written signatures.

I understand that the final assessment completed by the assessor(s) below will be sent to my eCredentials file and that I am given the option of activating my ecredentials file and, if I do, removing any documents that have been uploaded.

Assessor	**Assessor Signature***	**Assessor Address/Phone #**	**Date**
University Supervisor			
Mentor Teacher			
Student Teacher			

*The University supervisor, as designate, authenticates all signatures when uploading this document into eCredentials.

The Pennsylvania State University
College of Education

Performance-based Assessment of Student Teaching

Student
Teacher_______________________________________

Assessor____________________Title_____________________

Mid-term Assessment_________End Assessment_________

Date___________________________Date___________________

Domain A. Planning and Preparing for Student Learning

The Penn State student teacher plans instruction and assessments based upon robust understanding of subject matter, students and their learning and development, curriculum standards, and community and school context.

Planning Standard A1. The student teacher demonstrates

an understanding of subject matter and subject-specific pedagogy during planning.

Sample Indicators of Performance:

- Has a clear and accurate understanding of the content to be taught.
- Identifies important concepts and understandings to be learned.
- Sees connections among concepts, procedures, and applications.
- Uses appropriate resources to deepen own subject matter understanding.
- Anticipates potential for student misconceptions and difficulties with specific subject matter.

Rating: Standard A1

Consistently Often Sometimes Rarely Not Applicable

Planning Standard A2. The student teacher uses principles of learning and development, and understanding of learners and learner diversity during planning of instruction and assessment.

Sample Indicators of Performance:

- Considers and accommodates social, emotional, cognitive, and physical characteristics and needs of target learners in planning instruction.
- Ascertains and uses learner prior knowledge in planning instruction.
- Plans lessons and materials for learner diversity and background.

Rating: Standard A2

Consistently Often Sometimes Rarely Not Applicable

Planning Standard A3. The student teacher uses relevant community, district, school, and classroom factors and characteristics in planning.

Sample Indicators of Performance:

- When appropriate, uses local school or community resources in planning instruction.
- Uses knowledge of the local community to plan customized lessons or units for a specific classroom of students.

Rating: Standard A3

Consistently Often Sometimes Rarely Not Applicable

Planning Standard A4. The student teacher develops and selects appropriate instructional goals and objectives.

Sample Indicators of Performance:

- Lesson plans include clear goals written in the form of student learning outcomes.
- Lesson plans include learning goals that account for learner diversity and are challenging for all learners.
- Lesson plans identify goals that are achievable and permit measurable methods of assessment.
- Lesson plans identify goals that are based on appropriate local, state, and/or national academic standards.

Rating: Standard A4

Consistently Often Sometimes Rarely Not Applicable

Planning Standard A5. The student teacher designs coherent short range and long range opportunities for student learning and assessment.

Sample Indicators of Performance:

- Lesson plans include lesson goals, activities and assessments that are congruent with each other.
- Lesson plans for daily lessons are consistent with long-range instructional goals.

- Lesson plans sequence learning activities to maximize learning.
- Lesson plans include both formative and summative assessment opportunities.

Rating: Standard A5

Consistently Often Sometimes Rarely Not Applicable

Planning Standard A6. The student teacher selects, adapts, and/or creates appropriate instructional resources including instructional technologies.

Sample Indicators of performance:

- Selects/creates resources, materials, and technologies that match learning goals.
- Adapts materials as necessary to accommodate diverse learning needs.
- Uses technological resources to enhance student understanding of content when appropriate.

Rating: Standard A6

Consistently Often Sometimes Rarely Not Applicable

Planning Standard A7. The student teacher plans for a nurturing and supportive learning environment.

Sample Indicators of Performance:

- Plans a physical environment that accommodates needs of all learners.
- Plans a learning environment in which students feel safe and know what is expected.
- Plans specifically to enhance active student participation in lessons.
- Plans lessons that enable students to become more responsible for their own behavior.

- Plans classroom procedures and routines that are consistent with lesson goals and learning activities.

Rating: Standard A7

Consistently Often Sometimes Rarely Not Applicable

DOMAIN B: TEACHING

The Penn State student teacher encourages students' development and learning by creating a positive classroom learning environment and appropriately using a variety of instructional and assessment strategies and resources, including instructional technologies.

Teaching Standard B1. The student teacher actively and effectively engages all learners.

Sample Indicatioors of Performance:

- Links instructional activities to stu*dent perior knowledge and experience.*
- Adjusts instructional activities and provides alternative approaches in response to learner needs.
- uses questioning and discusion techniques that stimulate student thinking and participation.
- Uses motivational and reinforcement techniques that encourage engagement and intellectual risktaking.
- Demonstrates flexibility and responsiveness to unplanned or spontaneous events.

Rating: Standard B1

Consistently Often Sometimes Rarely Not Applicable

Teaching Standard B2. The student teacher assesses student learning in multiple ways in order to monitor student learning, assist students in understanding their progress, and report student progress.

Sample Indicators of Performance:

- Communicates to learners the role of assessment in the learning process.
- Provides assessment opportunities that capture student knowledge and ability in a variety of ways.
- Collects and analyzes relevant student data systematically and continuously.
- Uses assessment data to draw conclusions about the impact of teaching upon learners and adjusts instruction accordingly.
- Provides feedback to learners that is timely, accurate, specific, and constructive.
- Provides opportunities for students to use feedback in their learning activities.
- Maintains secure, accurate and pertinent student records

Rating: Standard B2

Consistently Often Sometimes Rarely Not Applicable

Teaching Standard B3. The student teacher appropriately manages classroom procedures.

Sample Indicators of Performance:

- Establishes/implements routines that effectively manage time and resources
- Communicates clear and consistent expectations
- Uses transitional time productively and effectively
- Uses instructional time productively and effectively
- Organizes the physical environment to support instructional activities
- Designs and uses an efficient system for handling non-instructional activities.

- Designs and uses a system for maintaining information on student completion of assignments and progress.

Rating: Standard B3

Consistently Often Sometimes Rarely Not Applicable

Teaching Standard B4. The student teacher appropriately manages student learning and behavior.

Sample Indicators of Performance:

- Communicates high academic and behavioral expectations.
- Communicates directions, procedures and expectations clearly and accurately.
- Demonstrates an awareness of student behavior
- Anticipates potential behavior problems and adjusts lessons to avoid them when possible.
- Responds appropriately to students' behavior, using a variety of direct and non-direct strategies such as proximity, eye contact, non-verbal cueing, etc.
- Establishes a culture that values learning as important student work.

Rating: Standard B4

Consistently Often Sometimes Rarely Not Applicable

Teaching Standard B5. The student teacher communicates effectively using verbal, nonverbal, and media communication techniques while teaching.

Sample Indicators of Performance:

- Speaks and writes correctly, effectively, and expressively
- Uses well-chosen, developmentally appropriate language that enriches lessons for all learners.
- Uses communications techniques that are relevant and sensitive to the learner and school context.

- Uses appropriate and effective questioning and discussion techniques.
- Uses media and technology appropriately to support student learning.

Rating: Standard B5

Consistently Often Sometimes Rarely Not Applicable

Domain C: Analyzing Student Learning and Inquiring into Teaching

The Penn State teacher examines student assessment data and continually and systematically inquires into the quality of his/her teaching and the conditions of schooling in order to enhance student learning and development.

Analyzing/Inquiring Standard C1. The student teacher monitors and adjusts instructional and assessment strategies during teaching.

Summary of Domain "B" - Teaching

Category	Exemplary	Good	Satisfactory	Needs Improvement	Unsatisfactory
Criteria for Rating	Performance consistently exceeds expectations. The vast majority of ratings on individual standards are "consistent."	Performance consistently meets and often exceeds expectations. Typical ratings are "often" with some ratings of "consistent"	Performance typically meets and occasionally exceeds expectations. Typical ratings are "often" or "sometimes"	Performance typically meets expectations but fails to meet expectations in an area or two. Typical ratings are "sometimes" with one or two "rarely"	Performance typically fails to meet expectations. Ratings of "rarely" are present in more than one or two areas or are so significant in one or more areas that overall performance is ineffective

Sources of evidence used to determine rating:

____ Lesson Plans ____ Unit Plan

____ Assessment Materials ____ Journal Entries

____ Portfolio ____ Observations (dates)

____ Other Assignment/Tasks

Comments to justify rating:

Sample Indicators of Performance:

- Uses formal and informal assessment to determine extent of student understanding of subject matter
- Makes modifications in instruction and assessment in response to student understanding
- Uses observations of student engagement and behavior to adjust instruction and assessment
- Capitalizes on "teachable moments" as appropriate

Rating: Standard C1

Consistently Often Sometimes Rarely Not Applicable

Analyzing/Inquiring Standard C2. The student teacher systematically analyzes assessment data to characterize performance of whole class and relevant sub-groups of students.

Sample Indicators of Performance:

- Collects assessment data systematically.
- Generates appropriate criteria for assessments.
- Determines patterns of student performance evident in the assessments for whole class.
- Can determine the extent to which each student has met learning outcomes.
- Reports on student achievement in appropriate ways to student, parents, and others.
- Can recommend "next steps" based on assessment data

- Selects specific alternative actions to re-teach challenging content.

Rating: Standard C2

Consistently Often Sometimes Rarely Not Applicable

Analyzing/Inquiring Standard C3. The student teacher uses data from his/her own classroom teaching to evaluate his/her own strengths and areas for improvement.

Sample Indicators of Performance:

- Conducts systematic inquiry into own teaching practices and acts upon self-analyses
- Makes thoughtful and accurate assessments of a lesson's effectiveness and the extent to which it achieved its goals
- Identifies strengths and limitations as a teacher, using examples from actual teaching performance
- Responds to supervision in a positive way to improve instruction
- Draws data-based conclusions about his/her effectiveness.

Rating: Standard C3

Consistently Often Sometimes Rarely Not Applicable

Domain D. Fulfilling Professional Responsibilities

The Penn State student teacher exhibits the highest standards of professionalism in all that s/he does. Professionalism Standard D1. The student teacher consistently meets expectations and fulfills responsibilities.

Summary of Domain "C" -- Inquiry and Analysis of Learning and Teaching

Category	Exemplary	Good	Satisfactory	Needs Improvement	Unsatisfactory
Criteria for Rating	Performance consistently exceeds expectations. The vast majority of ratings on individual standards are "consistent."	Performance consistently meets and often exceeds expectations. Typical ratings are "often" with some ratings of "consistent"	Performance typically meets and occasionally exceeds expectations. Typical ratings are "often" or "sometimes"	Performance typically meets expectations but fails to meet expectations in an area or two. Typical ratings are "sometimes" with one or two "rarely"	Performance typically fails to meet expectations. Ratings of "rarely" are present in more than one or two areas or are so significant in one or more areas that overall performance is ineffective

Sources of evidence used to determine rating:

____ Lesson Plans ____ Unit Plan

____ Assessment Materials ____ Journal Entries

____ Portfolio ____ Observations (dates)

____ Other Assignment/Tasks

Comments to justify rating:

Sample Indicators of Performance:

- Completes assignments and tasks accurately and with high quality
- Meets deadlines responsibly
- Fulfills commitments dependably and willingly
- Maintains an appropriate personal appearance
- Exhibits initiative, enthusiasm, and self-confidence

Rating: Standard D1

Consistently Often Sometimes Rarely Not Applicable

Professionalism Standard D2. The student teacher establishes and maintains productive, collaborative relationships with colleagues and families.

Sample Indicators of Performance:

- Views parents and families as partners in the education of their children.
- Communicates pertinent information about the instructional program and student progress with families, as appropriate.
- Shares ideas, information, skills and resources with colleagues in order to enhance the learning of all students.
- Demonstrates tactful, respectful interactions.
- Accepts opportunities to participate in extra-curricular, departmental activities when appropriate.

Rating: Standard D2

Consistently Often Sometimes Rarely Not Applicable

Professionalism Standard D3. The student teacher values and seeks professional growth.

Sample Indicators of Performance:

- Takes advantage of opportunities for professional development, such as attending workshops or conferences; procuring membership in a related professional organization; coaching or receiving coaching from a peer; making presentations to a school board or parents' group; leading a seminar discussion; conducting action research in a classroom.
- Takes responsibility for own learning.
- Seeks and uses educational research as a form of professional development.
- Possesses a growing repertoire of instructional and assessment strategies.
- Demonstrates ongoing growth in appropriate applications of technology.

Rating: Standard D3

Consistently Often Sometimes Rarely Not Applicable

Professionalism Standard D4. The student teacher continuously demonstrates integrity, ethical behaviors, and appropriate professional conduct.

Sample Indicators of Performance:

- Demonstrates professionalism as defined by the Pennsylvania Code of Professional Practice and Conduct for Educators.
- Demonstrates academic integrity and professionalism as defined by the University program and partnering school personnel.

- Demonstrates commitment to the highest professional standards when making decisions, solving problems, and safeguarding student records.
- Follows district and university policies, as well as state, local, and federal laws and regulations.

Rating: Standard – D4

Consistently Often Sometimes Rarely Not Applicable

Final Evaluation
Overall Rating

Student Teaching

Category	Exemplary	Good	Satisfactory	Unsatisfactory
Rating (indicate with an X)				

(Supervisor and Mentor both complete a letter of reference for final evaluation)

I acknowledge that I have read/prepared this assessment and discussed it with the appropriate party(ies).

Mid-Term Conference Date:

____

Final Conference Date:

____

Student Teacher__________________

Mentor Teacher__________________

University Supervisor______________

Summary of Domain "D"- Fulfilling Professional Responsibilities

Category	Exemplary	Good	Satisfactory	Needs Improvement	Unsatisfactory
Criteria for Rating	Performance consistently exceeds expectations. The vast majority of ratings on individual standards are "consistent."	Performance consistently meets and often exceeds expectations. Typical ratings are "often" with some ratings of "consistent"	Performance typically meets and occasionally exceeds expectations. Typical ratings are "often" or "sometimes"	Performance typically meets expectations but fails to meet expectations in an area or two. Typical ratings are "sometimes" with one or two "rarely"	Performance typically fails to meet expectations. Ratings of "rarely" are present in more than one or two areas or are so significant in one or more areas that overall performance is ineffective

Sources of evidence used to determine rating:

____ Lesson Plans ____ Unit Plan
____ Assessment Materials ____ Journal Entries
____ Portfolio ____ Observations (dates)
____ Other Assignment/Tasks

Comments to justify rating

APPENDIX D.

Guidelines for Using the Pennsylvania Statewide Evaluation Form for Student Professional Knowledge and Practice – Pennsylvania Department of Education—PDE-430

Heading and Signature Page

1. The heading of the evaluation form contains biographical information regarding you/candidate being evaluated and the evaluation period.
2. The subjects being taught and the grade level should be clearly listed.
3. Write the date on which the conference was held between you/candidate and the evaluator on the signature page of the PDE-430 form.
4. Clearly state the school year and the term in the appropriate place on the signature page.

Categories of Evaluation

1. PDE 430 has 4 major categories addressing evaluation of student teacher/candidate:

   i. Category I- Planning and Preparation

   ii. Category II- Classroom Environment

   iii. Category III-Instructional Delivery

   iv. Category IV-Professionalism

   Each category has student teacher/candidate performance indicators that support the category's evaluation on a continuum from Exemplary through Unsatisfactory.

The "Student Teacher/Candidate's Performance Appropriately Demonstrates" indicators are the criteria for the evaluation. Both the evaluator and you/candidate must be aware of the performance indicators being used in the evaluation before the evaluation takes place.

2. Each PDE 430 Category, I through IV, includes an explanation of the various aspects of teaching that aid in the further definition of the category.

Levels of Proficiency in the Categories

1. The categories presented on the PDE 430 provide knowledge, to the evaluator and you/candidate, of performance expectations and the required levels of proficiency for each category. The category's results, are evaluated through the review of the defined "Student Teacher/Candidate's Performance Demonstrates" indicators in each of the four categories.
2. You/candidate's demonstrated performance indicators in each category should be checked or highlighted in a manner to assist the evaluator in determining the appropriate level of proficiency. The judgment of the performance for the rating of any category is based on:

- The rater's overall evaluation of performance in each category and
- Is not dependent on seeing each single performance indicator demonstrated successfully in order to receive a high level evaluation.

Sources of Evidence

1. The sources of evidence, gathered by you and the evaluator, should be considered by the evaluator to make a judgment about your performance/level of proficiency.
2. It is also your responsibility to ensure the availability of evidence required for each of the categories evaluated.

The evaluator and you will share the sources at the conference date. The evaluator will mark, on the form next to the source of evidence, pertinent pieces of evidence that were reviewed during the evaluation of your performance/level of proficiency.

3. Since the evaluation form serves as a recordkeeping device in support of the recommendation for a successful performance assessment, it is important that the evaluator specify, next to the source of evidence, any evidence considered so that you, and other administrators reviewing the form, may have a sense of what was used to arrive at a judgment on the level of proficiency.
4. Sources of evidence should have, where appropriate, written dates that the source of evidence occurred: for example, the date of the planning document or dates of classroom observations/visits. Types of evidence reviewed can be listed as well as titles, for example, Back-to-School Night presentation. It should include the number of sources; for example if seven pieces of student work were collected for a particular source of evidence, that number should be included.
5. The space following each source of evidence allows an evaluator to document the important source(s) that were considered and captures the essential information about the source. If further space is required, an additional sheet may be attached.

Justification for Evaluation

1. After reviewing the results of your performance indicators in each category, and the pertinent sources of evidence, the assessor will make a judgment for each category on the PDE 430. The appropriate box is then checked.

2. This is a key section as it provides you with a clear understanding of the evaluator's decision based on observations and other specific sources of evidence. This section also provides further explanation of why you are receiving a particular rating for the category. The evaluator's comments help to focus you on your specific strengths and areas for improvement. It is important to write statements that are clear, consistent, and specify key areas for improvement, if required. The justification section may be expanded to whatever length the rater feels necessary to help you understand the rating, the reasons for it and steps that can be taken to improve performance, whenever required.

Evaluation

1. The evaluation/signature page of the PDE 430 includes the school year and term during which the observation occurred. An appropriate overall judgment of your demonstrated performance will be made and checked, resulting in a particular level of proficiency.
2. The signature of the evaluator, usually your supervisor, must be included. In addition, your signature and the appropriate signature dates must also be included. You do not have to agree with the judgments or statements of the evaluator in order to sign the form. You are obligated to sign the form once the evaluator has shared the contents of the form with you. You may annotate the form with "I disagree with this rating."
3. The Overall Justification for Evaluation section should specify any key areas for improvement, when used for the first assessment, and provide you with a clear understanding of the evaluator's overall judgment of the their performance. All written sections may be expanded in size in order to fully express the observations and recommendations to you.

Additional pages may be added if necessary.

The level of proficiency indicated in each of the 4 categories will added to determine an overall rating/level of proficiency for the entire PDE 430 form and the single rating period. At least a satisfactory rating must have been achieved in each of the 4 categories.

The certifying officer must now verify that the candidate has achieved at least a satisfactory rating on the PDE 430 by so indicating on the PDE 338C, College/University Verification Form, which is used to recommend a candidate to the Commonwealth for certification.

General Requirements

1. Each student teacher/candidate must be observed and evaluated using the PDE 430 a minimum of two times during their student teaching experience--once at the midpoint, and once at the end. Note that this is a minimum number of times and further evaluations may be completed, as the college/university desires. For example, if a candidate has two separate student teaching assignments, they may be observed at the midpoint and end of each assignment.
2. All evaluations with the PDE 430 are considered to be formative with the exception of the final one, which is considered to be the summative evaluation. All others are used in order to give you an opportunity to correct or improve any deficiencies. The PDE 430 assessment instrument must be used a minimum of two times. A satisfactory rating (1) in each of the 4 categories, resulting in a minimum total of at least (4) points, j must b eachieved on the final summative rating to favorably complete the overall assessment. Note that all categories must have achieved at least a satisfactory rating in all cases.
3. A copy of the PDE 430 is kept in the candidate's college file.You should have a copy of your completed PDE-430.

However, copies of the PDE 430 should not be provided by the college to outside agencies, prospective employers, or other individuals, in any situation, as this in an internal document. The PDE 430 is a confidential document. Copies of the PDE 430 will be reviewed during state major program reviews.

Division of Teacher Education

717-787-3470

Bureau of Teacher Certification and Preparation

Pennsylvania Department of Education (8/1/03)

APPENDIX E.

To Access The Pde 430 (The Pennsylvania Statewide Evaluation Form) You May Also Go To

http://www.teaching.state.pa.us/teaching/cwp/view.asp?a=90&pm=1&Q=32539

A viewing copy of the PDE 430 form is available on the following pages.

Please remember to use the student teacher's Penn State ID+ number when prompted to enter Social Security Numbers on all forms!!

Pennsylvania Statewide Evaluation Form (PDE 430) for Student Professional Knowledge and Practice.

Student/Candidate's Last Name________________________

First___________________________________

Middle__________________________________

Social Security Number____________________

Subject(s) Taught___________________________

Grade Level________________________________

This form is to serve as a permanent record of a student teacher/candidate's professional performance evaluation during a specific time period, based on specific criteria. This form must be used at least twice during the 12-week (minimum) student teaching experience.

Performance Evaluation

Directions: Examine all sources of evidence provided by the student teacher/candidate and bear in mind the aspects of teaching for each of the four categories used in this form. Check the appropriate aspects of student teaching, and indicate the sources of evidence used to determine the evaluation of the results in each category. Assign an evaluation for each of the four categories and then assign an overall evaluation of performance. Sign the form and gain the signature of the student teacher.

Category I: Planning and Preparation – Student teacher/candidate demonstrates thorough knowledge of content and pedagogical skills in planning and preparation. Student teacher makes plans and sets goals based on the content to be taught/learned, knowledge of assigned students, and the instructional context.
Alignment: 354.33. (1)(i)(A), (B), (C), (G), (H)

Student Teacher/Candidate's performance appropriately demonstrates:

- Knowledge of content
- Knowledge of pedagogy
- Knowledge of Pennsylvania's K-12 Academic Standards

- Knowledge of students and how to use this knowledge to impart instruction.
- Use of resources, materials, or technology available through the school or district
- Instructional goals that show a recognizable sequence with adaptations for individual student needs.
- Assessments of student learning aligned to the instructional goals and adapted as required for student needs.
- Use of educational psychological principles/theories in the construction of lesson plans and setting instructional goals.

Sources of Evidence (Check all that apply and include dates, types/titles and number)

- Lesson/Unit Plans____________________
- Resources/Materials/Technology____________________
- Assessment Materials____________________
- Information About Students____________________
  (Including IEP's)
- Student Teacher Interviews____________________
- Classroom Observations____________________
- Resource Documents____________________

Category	Exemplary 3 Points	Superior 2 Points	Satisfactory 1 Points	Unsatisfactory 0 Points
Criteria for Rating	The candidate *consistently* and *throughly* demonstrate indicators of performance	The candidate *usually and extensively* demonstrate indicators of performance	The candidate *sometimes and adequately* demonstrate indicators of performance	The candidate *rarely* or *never* and *inappropriately or superficially* demonstrates indicators of performance.
Rating (Indicate ✓)				

Justification for Evaluation

Justification for Evaluation

Student/Candidate's Last Name____________________

First____________________Middle______________

Social Security Number________________________

Category II: Classroom Environment – Student teacher/ candidate establishes and maintains a purposeful and equitable environment for learning, in which students feel safe, valued, and respected, by instituting routines and setting clear expectations for student behavior.

Alignment: 354.33. (1)(i)(E), (B)

Student Teacher/Candidate's performance appropriately demonstrates:

- Expectations for student achievement with value placed on the quality of student work.
- Attention to equitable learning opportunities for students.
- Appropriate interactions between teacher and students and among students.
- Effective classroom routines and procedures resulting in little or no loss of instructional time.
- Clear standards of conduct and effective management of student behavior.

- Appropriate attention given to safety in the classroom to the extent that it is under the control of the student teacher.
- Ability to establish and maintain rapport with students

Sources of Evidence (Check all that apply and include dates, types/titles, and number)

- Classroom Observations________________________
- Informal Observations/ Visits______________________
- Student Teacher/Candidate Interviews______________
- Visual Technology______________________________
- Resources/Materials/Technology/Space____________
- Other__________________________________

Category	Exemplary 3 Points	Superior 2 Points	Satisfactory 1 Point	Unsatisfactory 0 Points
Criteria for Rating	The candidate *consistently* and *thoroughly* demonstrate indicators of performance	The candidate *usually* and *extensively* demonstrate indicators of performance	The candidate *sometimes* and *adequately* demonstrate indicators of performance	The candidate *rarely* or *never* and *inappropriately or superficially* demonstrates indicators of performance.
Rating (Indicate ✓)				

Justification for Evaluation

Student/Candidate's Last Name________________________

First______________________Middle__________________

Social Security
Number_______________________________

Category III – Instructional Delivery - Student teacher/ candidate, through knowledge of content, pedagogy and skill in delivering instruction, engages students in learning by using a variety of instructional strategies.

Alignment: 354.33. (1)(i)(D),(F),(G)

Student Teacher/candidate's performance appropriately demonstrates:

- Use of knowledge of content and pedagogical theory through his/her instructional delivery.
- Instructional goals reflecting Pennsylvania K-12 standards.
- Communication of procedures and clear explanations of content.
- Use of instructional goals that show a recognizable sequence, clear student expectations, and adaptations for individual student needs.
- Use of questioning and discussion strategies that encourage many students to participate.
- Engagement of students in learning and adequate pacing of instruction.
- Feedback to students on their learning.
- Use of informal and formal assessments to meet learning goals and to monitor student learning.
- Flexibility and responsiveness in meeting the learning needs of students.
- Integration of disciplines within the educational curriculum.

Sources of Evidence (Check all that apply and include dates, types/titles, or number)

- Classroom

Observations________________________

- Informal Observations/Visits________________
- Assessment Materials______________________
- Student Teacher/Candidate Interviews_____________
- Student Assignment Sheets__________________
- Student Work________________________________
- Instructional Resources/Materials/Technology_______
- Other_________________________________

Category	Exemplary 3 Points	Superior 2 Points	Satisfactory 1 Point	Unsatisfactory 0 Points
Criteria for Rating	The candidate *consistently* and *thoroughly* demonstrate indicators of performance	The candidate *usually* and *extensively* demonstrate indicators of performance	The candidate *sometimes* and *adequately* demonstrate indicators of performance	The candidate *rarely* or *never* and *inappropriately or superficially* demonstrates indicators of performance.
Rating (Indicate ✓)				

Justification for Evaluation

Student/Candidate's Last Name____________________

First___________________Middle_______________

Social Security Number______________________

Category IV – Professionalism - Student teacher/candidate demonstrates qualities that characterize a professional person in aspects that occur in and beyond the classroom/building.

Alignment: 354.33. (1)(i)(I),(J)

Student Teacher/Candidate's performance appropriately demonstrates:

- Knowledge of school and district procedures and regulations related to attendance, punctuality and the like.
- Knowledge of school or district requirements for maintaining accurate records and communicating with families.
- Knowledge of school and/or district events.
- Knowledge of district or college's professional growth and development opportunities.
- Integrity and ethical behavior, professional conduct as stated in Pennsylvania Code of Professional Practice and Conduct for Educators; and local, state, and federal, laws and regulations.
- Effective communication, both oral and written with students, colleagues, paraprofessionals, related service personnel, and administrators.
- Ability to cultivate professional relationships with school colleagues.
- Knowledge of Commonwealth requirements for continuing professional development and licensure.

Sources of Evidence (Check all that apply and include dates, types/titles, or number)

- Classroom Observations________________________
- Informal Observations/Visits____________________
- Assessment Materials__________________________
- Student Teacher Interviews_____________________
- Written Documentation_________________________
- Student Assignment Sheets______________________
- Student Work______________________________

- Instructional Resources/Materials/Technology________
- Other____

Category	Exemplary 3 Points	Superior 2 Points	Satisfactory 1 Points	Unsatisfactory 0 Points
Criteria for Rating	The candidate *consistently* and *throughly* demonstrate indicators of performance	The candidate *usually and extensively* demonstrate indicators of performance	The candidate *sometimes and adequately* demonstrate indicators of performance	The candidate *rarely* or *never* and *inappropriately or superficially* demonstrates indicators of performance.
Rating (Indicate ✓)				

Justification for Evaluation

Overall Rating

Category	Exemplary 3 (Minimum of 12 Points)	Superior (Minimum of 8 Points)	Satisfactory 1 (Minimum of 4 Points)	Unsatisfactory (0 Points)
Criteria for Rating	The candidate *consistently* and *throughly* demonstrate indicators of performance	The candidate *usually and extensively* demonstrate indicators of performance	The candidate *sometimes and adequately* demonstrate indicators of performance	The candidate *rarely* or *never* and *inappropriately or superficially* demonstrates indicators of performance.
Rating (Indicate ✓)				

Note: This assessment instrument must be used a minimum of two times. **A satisfactory rating (1) in each of the 4 categories, resulting in a minimum total of at least (4) points, must be achieved on the final summative rating to favorably complete this assessment.**

Justification for Overall Rating:

Student Teacher/Candidate's Last Name________________

First____________________Middle____________________

Social Security Number_____________________________

District/IU______________School___________________

Interview/Conference Date__________________________

School Year:_______________Term:_________________

Required Signatures:

Supervisor/
Evaluator:_______________Date:_____________

Student Teacher
Candidate:__________Date:_____________

(Confidential Document)

APPENDIX F.

Penn State Mid-semester Goals and Strategies for the Second Half of the Semester

The student teacher will establish goals for continued growth and development during the second half of the semester at the mid-semester conference with the mentor teacher and university supervisor. The Penn State Teacher Education Performance Framework and Performance- Based Assessment are used as the bases for setting goals. Progress towards fulfillment of these goals will be reviewed and discussed at the final conference with the mentor teacher and university supervisor.

Domain A: Planning and Preparing for Student Learning

<u>GOALS</u>   <u>POSSIBLE STRATEGIES</u>

DOMAIN B: TEACHING

GOALS POSSIBLE STRATEGIES

Domain c. Analyzing student learning and inquiring into teaching.

GOALS POSSIBLE STRATEGIES

Domain D. Fulfilling Professional Responsibilities

GOALS POSSIBLE STRATEGIES

Signed ________________________Date ________________

APPENDIX G

Appendix G. Additional Discipline-specific Assessment Forms For Secondary Education Majors

Secondary and World Languange Student Teachers Also Will Be Assessed By Mentor Teachers And University Supervisors Through The Use of a Discipline Specific Assessment Form.

University Supervisors Will Provide Student Teachers With A Copy of the Appropriate Assessment Form.

The Discipline Specific Assessment Form is Applicable to Student Teachers in the Areas of:

English

Mathematics

Science

Social Studies

World Languages

APPENDIX H.

Hints for Mentors: Student Teacher Assessment

The following suggestions may be useful to the mentor teacher and University Supervisor as a guide in writing comments and/or letters of reference as required in completing the narrative section of the Final Assessment Summary.

- Describe briefly the setting of the placement assignment—grade, subject, or any other unusual facts which greatly affected the work of the student teacher
- Give both strengths and areas of need, being careful not to overdo either.
- Be careful to avoid blunt statements in presenting the areas of need of the student teacher.
- Make an honest judgment of student teacher presently and a reasonable prediction of his or her probable future development.
- Identify the type of situation in which the student teacher is most likely to succeed.
- Recall the student teacher's most outstanding achievement and try to make brief reference to it.
- Align comments to the PSU performance framework.

The following open-ended statements (Sandefer & Hinely,

Peabody Journal of Education, January, 1966) may prove helpful:

- The learning activities that ________ seem to direct most effectively were...
- The students' response to ________ was...
- ________'s ability to maintain effective classroom behavior was...
- ________ was particularly strong in his/her ability to...
- ________ could improve by strengthening competence in...
- Some activities ________ participated in other that student teaching were...
- ________'s ability to work effectively with other professional staff was...

The following global scale from the same source may offer additional help:

- ________ is making progress and shows promise; for his/her own good, however, it would probably be best if in his/her first position he/she could continue to receive close supervision and support for a while longer.
- ________ has done a reasonably good job, and I feel he/she is now competent to handle a classroom of his/her own satisfactorily.
- ________ has done a very good job. I am convinced he/she will be an asset to whatever school system may hire him/her; he/she may even become outstanding in time.
- ________ has done an unusually good job; with a little more opportunity for professional growth which will come from having a classroom of his or her own, he/she is almost

certain to become an outstanding teacher.

- ________ has done such an outstanding job that I believe right new he/she could step into any elementary/ secondary school in this area and be considered an outstanding teacher.

APPENDIX I.

Guidelines for Observation: Some Systematic Observation Techinques

Systematic observation entails using an instrument to collect data on an area of concern. In the student teaching experience the use of such an instrument allows a focused observation that could provide both you and the observer with valuable data. These data can then be used to promote further professional growth. The list of techniques below, followed by more detailed explanations for the use of each, suggests some of those that can be used for an area of concern:

I. Student Engaged Time Using a Seating Chart

Reasons used: Concern about "blind spots" in the room and knowing what all students are doing; concern about different types of student engagements during the lesson.

II. Verbal Flow—Class/Teacher Interaction/Wait Time

Reasons used: To determine type of class (lecture, discussion, other); to look at feedback provided by the teacher. Reason used: to determine amount of wait time used.

III. Modified Script Taping

Reason used: to compare lesson to the suggested steps in a lesson.

IV. Selected Verbatim

Reason used: to categorize teacher's questions according to Bloom's taxonomy or other verbal behaviors (SEE "Question/Task Chart" in APPENDIX M.)

V. Withall Social-emotional Climate Index

Reason used: to look at social-emotional climate in terms of teacher-centered or student centered classrooms.

VI. Teacher Clarity

Reason used: to determine whether teachers' questions, directions, and other verbal communications are clear.

VII. Teacher Enthusiasm

Reason used: to determine whether the teacher is displaying enthusiastic behavior.

The chart noted below suggests a method for choosing or designing a suitable instrument.

Creating Observation Records Decision Points

1. Specific behavior of interest?
2. Can it be stated in observable terms?
3. Which applies?:

   ____ Teacher behavior?

   ____ Large group behavior?

   ____ Individual student behavior?

   ____ Teacher and large group behavior?

   ____ Teacher and individual student behavior?

4. Time element, if yes:

   ____ Length of behavior?

   ____ Time sampling?

____ Exact time at which it occurs?

5. Sequence of behaviors, if yes:

   ____ Use sequential record?

   ____ Need sequential numbering system?

6. Will simple frequency count do?

7. Need some type of selective verbatim? If yes, which one?

8. Type of instrument needed?

   a. Frequency count

   b. Frequency count intervals

   c. Sequential record

   d. Sequential record intervals

   e. Seating chart

   f. Seating chart & teacher

   g. Seating chart with numbering

   h. Stopwatch and instrument

   i. Selective verbatim

   j. Other?

Systematic Observation Techniques

I. Student Engaged Time: Coding Categories

Category 1. Engaged	Coded with E.	Used for students who are engaged in the learning activity or attending to instruction.
Category 2. Management/ Transition	Coded with M.	Used for students who are taking part in daily routine activities like taking role, listening to directions.
Category 3. Socializing	Coded with S.	Used for students who are talking with each other about non-academic matters, passing notes, or watching others socialize.
Category 4. Discipline	Coded with D.	Used for students who are being reprimanded by teacher.
Category 5. Unengaged/ Observing	Coded with U.	Used for students who are sitting, standing, or walking with no evident purpose, playing with materials, staring into space, or other off-task behavior. This category is also used when behavior cannot be coded into any other category.
Category 6. Out of room	Coded with O.	Used for students who are out of the room for any purpose.

II. Verbal Flow: Coding Abbreviations

TS	Teacher statement (fact, opinion, direction)
TQ	Teacher question
RQ	Repeats/rephrases question
++	Praise
+	Affirms answer as correct
- (minus)	States answer is wrong
C	Criticizes answer
RA	Repeats student answer
FQ	Follow-up-question
SS	Student statement/answer
SQ	Student question
1	One second wait time

Procedure 1: If not interested in data on individual students, simply record each behavior as it occurs in sequence. Each sentence should be coded separately.

Procedure 2: If interested in data on individual students, simply record behaviors in the individual seating chart blocks. When using this procedure, each sentence is not coded. Each type of student or teacher behavior is given one code no matter how long the behavior lasts in terms of sentences.

III. Verbal Flow—Whole Class/Teacher Interaction/Wait Time

TS	Teacher statement	SV	Student volunteered
TQ	Teacher	SC	Student called on
TP	Teacher praise	SQ	Student question
TC	Teacher criticism	#=	Wait time in seconds

Sample Observation Sequence:

TQ SV TS TSTS TQ TS TS TQ 1.5 SC TS TSTS TQ SV SV TQ SC TS 1. 0 TQ TQTQ SC TS

IV. Example of Modified Script Taping

12:45 PM "Let's try to get back on track."

12:55 PM (students volunteering key terms) "perimeter" "area" "Go to third type of measurement." "volume"

12:58 PM "How do we use 'volume'?" Example: Using manipulatives, square units review, cubes (defined by student), "What do you mean by '3D'?", "To determine volume, we could use cubes."

1:01 PM putting cubes in a box; transfer to 10 cm sticks; transfer to 100 cm blocks; review of multiplication (multiples of 1000); checks for understanding

1:05 PM cube 10w x 10h x 10l = 1000 choral response

1:06 PM solid cube "What would you do?" (asking for transfer from cube to pencil box); multiply 1 x w x h; need to measure V = 1 x w x h (on board)

1:09 PM "How do we calculate area?"

Guided practice:

1:10 PM "Let's try some. How many cubes?"

1:11 PM second example; "How many cubes?" (worked through more examples together) Independent practice

1:21 PM (calculating the volume of a tractor trailer) "What do you do?" (5 volunteers) "How many others?" (3 additional hands) Called on volunteer, asked for agreement 1:25 PM worksheet

Closure (observation interrupted at this point)

V. Example of Selected Verbatim—Teacher Questions:

How would nature reduce the elements?

What do we call it when wind and water cut into rock?

What is working on it?

To where?

When it hits water, what happens?

What are some examples of organisms living a long time ago?

Does decaying create a fossil?

What creates it?

What decays?

What breaks down?

What else is there?

(See APPENDIX L. for an observation chart appropriate for use in analysis of questioning in conjunction with Bloom's Taxonomy.)

VI. Withall Social-emotional Climate Index By John Withall

A Frame of Reference and Procedure to Facilitate Categorization of Teacher-Statements.

Each teacher-statement contains one of two dominant kinds of intent. These are:

EITHER (a) intent to sustain the teacher and his behavior (teacher-centered statements)
Or (b) intent to sustain the learner and his behavior (learner centered statements and Issue-centered statements are included in this intent).

By analysis of both the CONTEXT and the CONTENT of a teacher-statement, it may be possible to determine whether the dominant intent of a statement is to sustain the teacher or the learner.

Once the dominant intent of the teacher-statement has been ascertained, one can proceed to determine the code by which the support is conveyed.

- If the statement is intended to sustain the teacher, one or possibly a combination of the two following codes may be used:
  - reproof of the learner (category 6)
  - directing or advising the learner (category 5)
  - Frequently the intent of the statement is to sustain the teacher yet neither of the above techniques is used. In that event the statement is simply a self-supportive remark that defends the teacher or evidence preservation in support of the teacher's position or ideas (category 7).
- If the intent of a statement is to sustain the learner then one or possibly a combination of the two following codes may be used:
  - clarification and acceptance of the learner's feelings or ideas (category 2), or
  - problem-structuring statements (category 3)
  - Frequently the intent of a statement is to sustain the learner yet neither of the above codes is used. In that event the statement is simply one that reassures, commends, agrees with, or otherwise sustains the learner (category 1).

Infrequently a teacher-statement may have no dominant intent to sustain either the teacher or the learner. If the statement represents neither of the categories in the two intent areas nor gives evidence of being one of the more general kinds of supporting statements, then the statement can be considered to have no intent to support and should be placed in category 4.

Recourse to the learner-statement or behavior before and after a teacher response, particularly when one encounters a statement in which the intent is difficult to ascertain, is sometimes helpful in categorizing the teacher's statements.

Criteria of Teacher Statement Categories

Category 1. LEARNER SUPPORTIVE statements or questions—these are teacher-statements or questions that express agreement with the ideas, actions, or opinions of the learner, or that commend or reassure the learner. Agreement is frequently expressed by a monosyllabic response such as "Yes,""Right," "Uhuhuh," and the like. Commendation or reassurances may be stated in terms of:

- Class-accepted criteria or goals, or
- The private goals and subjective criteria of the teacher.
  - The dominant intent of these statements or questions is to praise, encourage, or bolster the learner.
  - Examples of statements or questions in category 1 include:
- "That's fine, Bill, you've helped the class a lot."
- "Good for you, Joan."
- "Aren't you the one who brought in these excellent illustrations, Sam?"
- "How do you think up so many interesting comments?"

Category 2. Acceptant or Clarifying statements or questions—these are teacher-statements or questions which either:

- Accept, that is, evidence considerable understanding by the teacher of, or
- Clarify, that is, restate clearly and succinctly in the teacher's words the ideational or the feeling content of the learner's statement.

- The dominant intent of these teacher-responses is to help the learner gain insight into his problem, that is, define his "real" problem and its solution in more operation terms.
- Examples of statements or questions in category 2 include:
- "As you said, it's very complicated."
- "I know just how you feel. I get frustrated too when I work hard and long and get nowhere."
- "If I understand you rightly, we should take the square root, sum the means, and finally divide by 100 to find the proportion."
- "As I get it, you'll analyze the historical facts from McCauley's history, add the material that you got from Waverly's chapters, and wind up with your concluding paragraph."

Category 3. PROBLEM-STRUCTURING statements or questions—these are responses by the teacher that offer facts, ideas, or opinions to the learner about:

- Phenomena, and
- Procedures
  - ➢ Presented in a non-threatening and objective manner. These responses contain NO elements of advising or recommending the adoption of certain ideas or procedures. Problem-structuring responses are frequently posed as questions which seek further information from the learner about the problem confronting him; or they may be statements which offer information to the learner about his problem. The learner is free to accept or to reject in part or in entirety the facts or opinions that are presented to him. Problem-structuring responses may be

questions which the teacher asks 1) to further increase his own understanding of what the learner has said, or 2) to increase the precision of the learner's statement of the problem. Problem-structured responses are problem-centered rather than either teacher- or learner-centered; nevertheless, they do tend to sustain the learner by facilitating his problem-solving activities.

- Examples of statements or questions in category 3 are:
  - "What is the distance of the moon from the earth?"
  - "What is the formula for finding the area of a circle?
  - "Do a feather and lump of lead fall at the same speed in a vacuum?"
  - "Sound travels at approximately 700 miles per hour in the air."

Category 4. NEUTRAL statements evidencing no supportive intent.

- Statements are neither teacher-sustaining, nor learner-sustaining, nor problem-centered. They constitute a small percentage in which the teacher:
  - questions himself aloud;
  - repeats verbatim a statement that the learner just made;
  - uses a polite formality, et cetera. Statements having to do with administrative procedure—the room in which the class will meet, the hour at which a conference will occur—(especially after consensus has been achieved), fall into this category.
  - Examples of statements or questions in category 4 are:

- "We were looking at page 212 yesterday."
- "I'm sorry, I didn't quite catch what you said."
- "May I help?"
- "Let's meet at noon tomorrow."
- "Please excuse my clumsiness."

Category 5. DIRECTIVE statements or questions

- These are teacher-statements or questions which advise the learner regarding a course of action or his behavior and which narrowly limit his choice or offer no choice. These statements recommend to the learner the facts or procedures that the teacher proffers him. These statements or questions convey the impression to the learner that the teacher expects and hopes that he will follow his prompting and that he will approve if he does. The intent of these responses is to have the learner take up the teacher's point of view and pursue a course of action that he advocates.
  - ➢ Examples of statements or questions in category 5 are:
    - "That's to be in by the twelfth without fail."
    - "Why not do it the way I recommended in the first place?"
    - "That's to be completed before you leave."
    - "I'd appreciate your doing it in accordance with the proposed outline."

Category 6. Reproving, Disapproving, or Disparaging statements or questions.

- By means of these statements a teacher may express a complete or partial disapproval of the ideas, behavior, and to him, personality weaknesses of the learner. The teacher's internalized societal values largely enter into these responses. By means of these statements some teachers believe they are fulfilling their responsibility in inculcating in your people society's standards of acceptable and desirable behavior and achievement. The intent of these statements is:

- To represent to the learner societal values as the teacher sees them.
- To admonish the learner for unacceptable behavior and to deter him from repeating it in the future.
- To impress on the learner the fact that he has not met the criteria for successful achievement which the teacher accepts.
- Examples of statements or questions in category 6 are:
  - "You people are always griping about something."
  - "If you had listened you would have heard."
  - "Why don't you buckle down and get to work for a change?"
  - "That's a stupid question."
  - "You mean to say that's all you did?"
  - "Considering you did it, that's not bad."

Category 7. Teacher-supportive statements or questions

- These are statements or questions in which the teacher refers to himself and expresses a defensive attitude, or refers to his present or past interests, activities, or possessions with the purpose of reassuring himself and of confirming his position or his ideas in the eyes of those around him. The dominant intent of these teacher responses is to assert, defend, or justify the teacher. Statements in which the teacher perseverates on an idea, a belief, or a suggestion would fall into this category. By "perseveration" is meant a persisting in, a reiteration of, and a rigid advocacy of an idea or opinion by the teacher despite additional data being presented to him which calls for a reexamination of the original idea or opinion. Examples of statements or questions in category 7 are:

- "You know as well as I do that I don't make unreasonable demands."
- "Aren't my questions usually clear and concise though?"
- "I extended myself especially to suit your convenience."

Social Emotional Climate Index
by John Withall

Category 1. Praise
Category 2. Acceptant/Clarifying
Category 3. Problem Structuring
Category 4. Neutral
Category 5. Directive
Category 6. Preprimands
Category 7. Teacher Defensive

<table>
<tr><td>1</td><td>2</td><td>3</td><td>4</td><td>5</td><td>6</td><td>7</td></tr>
<tr><td></td><td></td><td></td><td></td><td></td><td></td><td></td></tr>
<tr><td></td><td></td><td></td><td></td><td></td><td></td><td></td></tr>
<tr><td colspan="4">1 +2 + 3 = Learner Centered</td><td colspan="3">5 + 6 + 7 = Teacher Centered</td></tr>
</table>

VII. The Clear Teacher Checklist

As your teacher, I hope I am clear. In order to improve my ability to be clear I need your help. Below are 28 statements that describe what clear teachers do. Read each statement and place a check mark in the column that tells how often I perform the behavior that is described. In that way I'll know what I do well and what I need to improve. (Put a check mark in one box after each statement.

As our teacher, you:	All of the time	Most of the time	Some of the time	Never	Does of apply
1. Explain things simply					
2. Give explanations we understand					
3. Teach at a pace that is not too fast and not too fast and not too slow.					
4. Stay with a topic until we understand it.					
5. Try to find out when we don't understand and then you repeat things.					
6. Teach things step-by-step.					
7. Describe the work to be done and how to do it.					
8. Ask if we know what to do and how to do it.					
9. Repeat things we don't understand.					
10.Ecplain something and thenwork.					
11.Explain something and then stop so we can ask questions.					
12.Prepare us for what we will be doing next.					
13.Give specific details when teaching.					
14.Repeat things that hard to understand.					

15. Work examples and explain.					
16. Give us a chance to think about					
17. Explain something and then stop so we can think about it.					
18. Show us how to do the work.					
19. Explain the assignment and the materials we need to do.					
20. Strees difficult points.					
21. Show examples of how to do classroom and homework.					
22. Give us enough time for practice.					
23. Answer our question.					
24. Ask question to find out if we understand.					
25. Go over difficult homework problems.					
26. Shoe us how to remember things.					
27. Explain how to do assignments by using examples.					

"The Clear Teacher Checklist" is based substantially on research findings contained in the article by Kennedy, et al. in Journal of Educational Research, Sept./Oct., 1978.

VII. Teacher Enthusiasm

Directions: To determine your enthusiasm level, videotape several lessons, then rate yourself. Avoid rating only one lesson. A score of 8-20 indicates an unenthusiastic level, 21-42 indicates a moderate level of enthusiasm, and 43-56 indicates a very high level of enthusiasm.

Teacher Behavior Regarding	1 Low	2	3 Medium	4	5 High
Vocal Delivery from whisper; many	Monotonous Voice, minimum vocal inflection; little variations in speed of speech; drones on and on; ; drones		Pleasant variations of pitc, volume and speed; good articulation		Great and sudden changes rapid excited speech to a varied uplifting intonation;
Eyes	Looks dull or bored; seldom opens eyes wide or raises		Appears Interested; occasionally light up, shining, opening wide.		Characterized as danxing, snapping lighting up frequently opening wide; eyebrows. occasiionally raised.
Gestures	Seldom moves arms out or stretches out towards person or object; never uses sweeping movement; keeps arms at side or folds across body; appears rigid.		Often points with hand, using total arm; occasionally uses sweeping motion using body, head, arms, hands and face; steady pace of gesturing is maintained.		Quick and demonstrative movement of body, head, arms, hands, and face(e.g., clapping hands, head nodding hands, head nodding rapidly).
Facial Expressions	Appears deadpan; does not denote feeling; frowns most of the time; little smiling or a one-second lip upturn; lips upturn; lips closed.		Agreeable; smiles frequently longer and at a regular rate; looks pleased happy/sad when obviously called for.		Appears vibrant, demonstrative; shows surprise awe sadness joy thought fulness excitement; total smile with mouth open; quick and sudden changes in expression.

Body Movement	Seldom movves from one spot or movement mainly from a sitting to a stand ing positiion.	Moves freely, slowly, and steadily.	arge body movement; swings around; walks rapidly; changes pace; unpredictable; energetic
Word Selection	Mostly nouns, few descriptors/adjectives	Some descriptors/adjectives or repetition of the same ones	Highly descriptive; many adjectives; great variety.
Acceptance of Ideas and Feelings	Little indication of acceptance or encouragement; may lignore pupil's feelings or ideas.	Accepts ideas and feeling praises or clarifies; some variation in response but frequently repeats same variation in response but frequently repeats same ones.	Quick and ready to give praise and encouragement for ideas and feeling clarifies willingly and easily; many variations in response; vigorous nodding of head when agreeing.
Overall Energy	Lethargic; appears inactive, dull or sluggish.	Some variations from high to low in appearingenergetic; demonstrative but mostly an even level is maintained.	Exuberant; maintains high degree of energy and vitality; highly demonstrative; great and sudden changes in voice, tone, pitch eye, head, arm and body movement.

Adapted from: Mary Lynn Collins, "The Effects of Training for Enthusiasm of the Enthusiasm Displayed by Preservice Elementary Teachers, "Teachers," 1976.

.**Adapted from:** Mary Lynn Collins, "The Effects of Training for Enthusiasm of the Enthusiasm Displayed by Preservice Elementary Teachers," 1976.

APPENDIX J.

Orientation to School Assignment

Name _______________School ___________________

Student teachers are advised to not interrupt the mentor teacher, principal, secretary, etc., too much during the first few days of the semester. It is good practice to request an appointment after as much as possible has been completed alone or with a peer.

I. Basic Information: Check off as completed

Ask for a printed plan of the school.

Identify your classroom. Draw in the emergency exit route. Walk the emergency route.

Determine your class schedule.

Identify your teacher's responsibilities/obligations (teaching by subject, cafeteria duty, etc).

Obtain a class roster and seating plan.

Become familiar with names, nicknames, abbreviations and pronunciations.

Review Student Handbook and Teacher Handbook, if these exist.

Review all policies and procedures.

II. Physical Plan and School Personnel: Check off as completed and locate the following, mark on school map, and introduce self where appropriate.

Your assigned classroom.

Other teachers in the same grade/department /subject

(get teachers' names)
The students' restrooms—boys and girls
The teachers' lounge(s).
The teachers' restrooms—men's and women's
The secretary's office. His/Her name:
The guidance counselor's office. His/Her name:
The nurse's room. His/Her name:
The principal's office. His/Her name:
The custodians' office. Their names:
The pay telephone.
The special rooms and specialists' names.
(a) all purpose
(b) art
(c) auditorium
(d) before-and after-school program
(e) counselor
(f) ELL
(g) Gifted
(h) gym
(i) tech ed
(j) library
(k) music
(l) other
(m) planetarium
(n) Resource Room
(o) Science
(p) swimming pool
(q) other
(r) cafeteria and cafeteria workers' names:

III. Non -Instructional Duties: note the answers to the questions below.

When and where are faculty meetings?
What time do they start? End?
Teachers must be in their classrooms by:
Teachers must stay until:
Time students begin arriving :
Time Students leave :
Where do buses drop off and pick up?
When does the school day formally begin?
When are the P.A. announcements made?
When is/are recess(es)?
Where may the students play at recess?
Students may stay in at recess/lunch for the following reasons:
Who supervises the students during outdoor recess?
During indoor recess?
What time is lunch for the school?
What time is lunch for your grade/teacher?
Do you need a lunch account to buy lunch?
Who accompanies students to specials/programs/classes?
Who returns students to their classes?
Where may students wait for parents?
What are the procedures/regulations regarding driving to school?
What other non-teaching duties does your mentor teacher have?
What non-teaching duties will you participate in?

IV. Services in the School: make note of answers to the following questions.

Supplies for use in the classroom

What procedures should you follow?

What is available for your use?

Making copies, laminating, computers, etc.

Where?

What kind of machines?

Can you operate them without assistance?

Procedures and rules for their use?

Computers

Do you need a computer account?

How to reserve computer lab?

Procedures, rules, and expectations for use?

Audio-visual supplies

Where?

How do you order/acquire videos, slides, computer software/hardware?

Procedure and rules

How much notice to order?

Are supplies available from the I.U.?

Secretarial and related assistance

What assistance is available to you?

Is prior notice needed?

What are guidelines for office use, protocol, and etiquette?

Janitorial and other assistance

What procedures should you be aware of?

V. Emergency Procedures: make note of critical information

What happens in an emergency drill?

Under what conditions does the building get evacuated?

What is the exit route and alternate route?

What are the emergency rules and procedures?

Which radio/TV stations/web sites carry the school delays/ cancellations?

How will you know when your school is delayed or canceled?

Who will contact you in case of a school closing (e.g., snow chain or telephone tree)?

What are the school cancellation procedures?

How do they involve you?

Which of your students have special needs that might require emergency care (e.g., medical, allergies, psychological)?

What are the procedures for student health emergencies?

Ask about universal precautions.

V1. Teaching Information

Homework

Collect and review carefully curriculum guides and student texts.

What are the school district homework guidelines for your grade?

Where are homework assignments posted?

Do the students copy down assignments? When and to where?

How do the parents know what the assignments will be?

Must the parents sign anything? If so, what?

When is homework checked and/or collected?

What happens if homework is not completed?

Other information regarding homework:

Student Records

What is the school district's policy regarding records kept on the students?

Where are they kept?

Grade Book

What is recorded?

Procedures?

What is your role?

Will you keep grades for the classes you teach?

Will you use your own grade book/spreadsheet?

Classroom Procedures

Obtain specific classroom rules/regulations

How are passes handled?

How are absences/tardies handled?

Co-curricular activities

When?

Where?

VII. Other

Student teachers should make note of other information that may be of assistance during the student teaching assignment.

Some examples include field trip policies, policies regarding photographing and video taping of students, unauthorized parent visits, drug and alcohol problems and policies, sex education, student assistance programs, inclusion, gifted and talented programs, in-service, conferencing policies, etc.

APPENDIX K.

Principles of Learning

Student teachers should refer to the following principles as they plan, implement and analyze instruction. A student teacher may discover that instruction was less effective than he or she had hoped because consideration was not given to one or more of these principles. Or, one might discover, happily, that instruction was more effective because the principles of learning were considered.

1. Positive reinforcement is more likely to result in learning than negative reinforcement or punishment.
2. Reinforcement is most effective when it occurs immediately following the appropriate behavior.
3. Short practice sessions held more frequently are more effective than fewer long-term sessions.
4. Learning is more effective if the students show "readiness" for what is to be learned.
5. Learning generally proceeds more easily if information is presented in order from simple to complex, familiar to unfamiliar, and tangible to abstract.
6. The learner learns other things besides what the teacher is formally presenting.
7. Learners learn best by being actively involved.
8. More complex skills develop more slowly than simple skills.
9. Learning is increased if time is spent on recalling what has been read.
10. Detail must be placed in structured patterns or it is rapidly forgotten.
11. Material that is made meaningful to the learner is more easily learned and better retained than irrelevant material.
12. Disequilibrium--or a perceived discrepancy--promotes learning because the learner naturally seeks to resolve the discrepancy and reach a new equilibrium.
13. Interaction enhances many types of learning.

14. Learning is enhanced in a supportive, non-threatening atmosphere.
15. Learning is increased by a rich and varied environment.
16. Learning is enhanced when a single concept is related to a wide variety of experiences.

Adapted from Travers, R.M.W. (1982). Essentials of Learning Macmillan Publishers.

APPENDIX L.

Planning Resources
Bloom's Taxonomy
(Cognitive Domain for Teaching)

It is critical for educators to address all cognitive levels of the students through our instruction, challenging ourselves to challenge them in their thinking and their production. A way to "check ourselves" to see that we are reaching each of these levels, is to build in appropriate performance tasks for them in our lessons. Consider the use of Bloom's Taxonomy to assist in the development of lesson plans. Listed below are the six levels of cognition that Bloom has addressed, and explanation of each, and a suggested list of "verbs" to use in the directions for the performance task given the students.

KNOWLEDGE—represents the lowest level of objectives. The definition of knowledge for this level is remembering previously learned material. The requirement is simple recall. The range of information may vary from simple facts to complex theories, but regardless of the complexity, knowledge is the cognitive level being utilized by the brain.

Examples of verbs or phrases to use to direct the desired learning task include: define, fill in the blank, identify, label, list, locate, match, memorize, name, spell, state, tell, and underline.

COMPREHENSION—is the first step beyond simple recall. It is the first level at which we see demonstration and understanding of information. It is the ability to apprehend, grasp, and interpret the meaning of material.

Examples of verbs or phrases to use to direct the desired learning task include: convert, describe, explain, interpret, paraphrase, put in order, restate, retell in your own words, rewrite, and summarize.

APPLICATION—is the ability to show the pertinence of principles to different situations. At this level, students may apply concepts or methods to actual concrete problems. This thinking skill tells that a student can transfer selected information to a life problem or a new task with a minimum of direction.

Examples of verbs or phrases to use to direct the desired learning task include: compute, conclude, construct, demonstrate, determine, draw, give an example, illustrate, make, show, and solve.

ANALYSIS—requires more than knowledge, comprehension, and application. It also requires an understanding of the underlying structure of the material. Analysis is the ability to break down material to its functional elements for better understanding of the organization. Analysis may include identifying parts and clarifying relationships among parts. This thinking skill tells that a student can examine, take apart, classify, predict, and draw conclusions.

Examples of verbs or phrases to use to direct the desired learning task include: categorize, classify, compare, contrast, debate, deduct, determine the factors, diagnose, diagram, examine, and specify.

SYNTHESIS—requires the formulation of new understandings. If analysis stresses the parts, synthesis stresses the whole. Components of concepts may be reorganized into new patterns and new wholes. A student can originate, combine, and integrate parts of prior knowledge into a new product, plan, or proposal.

Examples of verbs or phrases to use to direct the desired learning task include: change, combine, compose, construct, create, design, find an unusual way, formulate, generate, invent, predict, produce, pretend, rearrange, reorganize, suggest, and visualize.

EVALUATION—is the highest level of learning results in the hierarchy. It includes all the other levels plus the ability to make judgment, assess, or criticize based on evidence and clearly defined criteria. Examples of verbs or phrases to use to direct the desired learning task include: appraise, choose, compare, conclude, decide, defend, evaluate, give your opinion, judge, justify, prioritize, rank, rate, select, support, and value.

Teaching Secondary School Science: Strategies for Developing Scientific Literacy. NJ: Prentice-Hall.

Wong, H., & Wong, T. (1998). How to be an Effective Teacher: The First Days of School. CA: Harry K. Wong Publications.

II. Where Do Questions & Performance Tasks Fall?

There is an art to asking questions. You should ask questions that are clear, logically sequenced, and adapted to the level of the learners, (Goethals, et. al., 2004). The types of performance tasks we have students perform are equally important to their level of learning. As beginning teachers, we should consider making use of a chart similar to the one below, recording a sampling of the questions and/or performance tasks we ask of our students, either during instruction or assessment. Referring to the information on Bloom's Taxonomy on the previous page, we can determine which cognitive level our question/tasks address, making an effort to develop those that incorporate all levels of thinking.

Question/ Performance Tasks	Knowl -edge	Compre- hension	Applic -ation	Anal- ysis	Synt- hesis	Evalua -tion

The best use of this chart is to record all anticipated questions or tasks for a particular lesson and determine the cognitive range of questioning and performance, as well as their frequency at specific levels. It is also an excellent planning tool for preparing assessment questions and tasks.

The idea for the chart is credited to:

Goethals, M., et. al. (2004). Student Teaching: A Process Approach to Reflective Practice. NJ: Pearson, Merrill Prentice Hall.

References / Suggested Readings

Acheson, K.A. & Gall, M.D. (1987), Techniques in the clinical supervision of teachers (2nd ed.). New York: Longman.

Armaline, W.D. & Hoover, R.L. (1989). Field experiences as a vehicle for transformation: Ideology, education, and reflective practice. Journal of Teacher Education. 12(1). 42-48.

Blank, M.A. & Heathington, B.S. (1987). The supervisory process: A consistent approach to help student teachers improve. Teacher Educator. 22(4). 2-14.

Bolin, F.S. (1988). Helping student teachers think about teaching. Journal of Teacher Education. 39 (2), 48-55.

Bolin, F. and Panaritis, P (1992). Searching for a common purpose: A perspective on the history of, supervision. In C. Glickman (Ed.), Supervision in Transition (pp. 30-43). Alexandria, VA: Association for Supervision and Curriculum

Development.

Christensen, P.S. (1988). The nature of feedback student teachers receive in postobservation conferences with the university supervisor: A comparison with O'Neal's study of cooperating teacher feedback. Teaching and Teacher Education. 4. 275-286.

Cogan, M. (1973). Clinical Supervision. Boston: Houghton Mifflin.

Cohn, M.M. & Gellman, V.C. (1988). Supervision: A developmental approach for fostering inquiry in preservice teacher education. Journal of Teacher Education. 39(2)t 2-8.

Colton, A.B. & Sparks-Langer, G. (1992). Restructuring student teaching experiences. In C.D.

Glickman, (Ed.). Supervision in transition (pp. 155-168). Alexandria, VA: Association for Supervision and Curriculum Development.

Conant, J.B. (1963). The education of American teachers. New York: McGraw Hill.

Copeland, W.D. (1980). Student teachers' preference for supervisory approach. Journal of Teacher Education. 33(2). 32-36.

Cruickshank, D.R. (1985). Models for the preparation of America's Teachers. Bloomington, IN: Phi Delta Kappa Educational Foundation.

Danielson, C.(1996). Enhancing professional practice: A framework for teaching (rev ed.) Alexandria, VA: Association for Supervision and Curriculum Development.

Danielson, C. & McGreal, T. (2000). Teacher evaluation to enhance professional practice. Alexandria, VA: Association for Supervision and Curriculum Development

Doyle, W. (1996) Classroom organization and management. In M. Wittrock (Ed.) Handbook of research on teaching (3rded.)(pp.392-431). New York: Macmillan.

Firth, G., & Pajak, E. (Eds.) (1998). Handbook of research on school supervision. New York: Macmillan Library Reference.

Gagne, E.D.(1985). The cognitive psychology of school learning. Boston: Little, Brown and Company.

Garman, N.B. (1986). Reflection, the heart of clinical supervision: A modern rationale for professional practice. Journal of Curriculum and Supervision. 2(3). 2.

Garman, N. (1986). The clinical approach to supervision. In T.J. Sergiovanni (Ed.), Supervision of teaching (pp 35-52). Alexandria, VA: Association for Supervision and Curriculum Development.

Glassburg, S. & Sprinthall, N.A. (1980). Student teaching: A developmental approach. Journal of Teacher Education. 31(2). 31-38.

Glickman, CD. (1981). Developmental supervision: Alternative Practices for helping-teachers improve instruction. Alexandria, VA: Association for Supervision and Curriculum Development.

Glickman, CD. & Bey, T.M. (1990). Supervision. In W.R. Houston (Ed.), Handbook of research on teacher education (pp. 549-566). New York: Macmillan.

Goethals, M., et. al. (2004). Student Teaching: A Process Approach to Reflective Practice. NJ: Pearson, Merrill Prentice Hall.

Goldhammer, R. (1969) Clinical supervision: Special techniques for the supervision of teachers. New York: Holt, Rinehart and Winston.

Goldhammer, R., Anderson, R.H. & Krajewski, R.J. (1980). Clinical supervision. (2nd ed.). New York, Holt, Rinehart and Winston.

Goodlad, J. (1983). Teachers for our nation's schools, San

Francisco, CA: Jossey-Bass, Inc.

Goodlad, J.I., Soder, R., Sirotnik, K.A. (Eds.), (1990). Places where teachers are taught. San Francisco: CA: Jossey-Bass, Inc.

Goodlad, J.I., Soder, R., Sirotnik, K.A. (Eds.), (1990). The moral dimensions of teaching. San Francisco, CA: Jossey-Bass, Inc.

Goodman, J. (1983). The seminar's role in the education of student teachers: A case study. Journal of Teacher Education. 34(3). 44-49.

Griffin, G. (1986). Issues in student teaching: A review. In J.D. Raths & L.G. Katz (Eds.), Advances in teacher education, (Vol. 2, pp. 239-273). Norwood, NJ: Ablex.

Grimmett, P.P. & Ratzlaff, H.C. (1986). Expectation for the cooperating teacher role. Journal of Teacher Education, 37(6). 41-50.

Guyton, E.G. & Mclntrye, D.J. (1990). Student teaching and school experiences. In W.R. Houston (Ed.),

Handbook of research on teacher education (pp. 514-534). New York: Macmillan.

Henry, M.A. & Beasley, WW (1989). Supervising student teachers in a professional way (2nd ed.).

Terre Haute, IN: Sycamore Press.

Holmes Group (1986). Tomorrow's Teachers. East Lansing, MI: Author.

Hoover, L.A. (1994). Reflective writing as a window on preservice teachers' thought processes. Teaching and Teacher Education, 10(1), 83-93.

Hoover, N.L., O'Shea, L.J. &Carroll, R.G. (1988). The supervisor intern relationship and effective interpersonal communication skills. Journal of Teacher Education. 39(2). 22-27.

Hunter, M. (1984). Knowing, teaching, and supervising.

In P.L. Hosford (Ed.), Using what we know about teaching (pp. 169-193). Alexandria, VA: Association for Supervision and Curriculum Development.

Joyce, B & Weil, M. (1986). Models of teaching (Third Edition). Englewood Cliffs, NJ: Prentice-Hall, Inc.

Kagan, D.M. & Albertson, L.M. (1987). Student teaching: Perceptions of supervisory meetings. Journal of Education for Teaching. 13(1). 49-60.

Kilbourn, B. (1984), Linda: A case study in clinical supervision. In W. John Smyth (Ed.), Case studies in clinical supervision. Geelong, Australia: Deakin University Press.

Levin, J. & Nolan, J. F. (1996). Principals of classroom management: A professional decision-making model (2nd ed.). Needham Heights, MA: Allyn & Bacon.

Nolan, J.F. (1997). Can a supervisor be a coach? In J. Glantz & R. Neville (Eds.), Educational supervision: Perspectives, issue and controversies (pp.100-108). Norwood, MA: Christopher Gordon

Nolan, J.F. & Hoover, L. A. (2004). Teacher Supervision and Evaulation. Hoboken, NJ: John Wiley and Sons

Nolan, J.F. & Huber, T. (1989). Nurturing the reflective practitioner through instructional supervision. Journal of Curriculum and Supervision. 4(2). 126-145.

Peterson, K. (2000). Teacher evaluation: A comprehensive guide to new direction and practices. Thousand Oaks, CA: Corwin.

Posner, G. J. (1996). Field experience: A guide to reflective teaching (4th ed.). New York: Longman Publishers.

Reynolds, M.C. (Ed.). (1989). Knowledge base for the beginning teacher. New York: Pergamon Press.

Richardson-Koehler, V. (1988). Barriers to the effective supervision of student teaching: Afield study. Journal of Tbacher Education. 39(2). 28-35.

Robinson, J. (1984). A second pair of eyes: A case study of a supervisor's view of clinical supervision. In W, John Smyth (Ed.), Case studies in clinical supervision. Geelong, Australia: Deakin University Press.

Rust, F.O. (1988). How supervisors think about teaching. Journal of Tbacher Education, £9(2), 56-64. Schon, D.A. (1983). The reflective practitioner: How professionals think in action. New York: Basic Books.

Schon, D.A. (1987). Educating the reflective practitioner: Toward a new design for teaching and learning in the professions. San Francisco, CA: Jossey-Bass, Inc.

Shon, D. (1988). Coaching reflective teaching. In P.P. Grimmet & G.L. Erickson (Eds.) Reflection in teacher education. New York: Teachers College Press

Sergiovanni, T.J., & Starratt, R.J. (2002) Supervision: A redefinition(6th ed.). Boston: McGraw-Hill.

Smyth, J, (1984). Clinical supervision - Collaborative learning about teaching. Geelong, Australia: Deakin University Press.

Smyth, W.J. (1989). Developinpg and sustaining critical reflection in teacher education. Journal of Teacher Education, 40(2), 2-9.

Thies-Sprinthall, L. (1986). A collaborative approach for mentor training: A working model. Journal of Tbacher Education. 37(6). 13-20.

Zahorik, J.A. (1988). The observing-conferencing role of university supervisors. Journal of Tbacher Education. 39 (2), 9-16.

Zeichner, KM. (1981). Reflective teaching and field-based experience in teacher education. Interchange. 12(1). 5-24.

Zeichner, K. (1982). The belief systems of university supervisors in the elementary student teaching program. Journal of Education for Teaching. 8(1). 34-54.

Zeichner, K.M. & Liston, D.P. (1987). Teaching student teachers to reflect. Harvard Educational Review. 57(1). 23-48.

Zeichner, K.M. & Liston, D.P. (1996). Reflective teaching: An introduction. Mahwah, NJ: Erlbaum.

Zimpher, W.L., deVoss, G.G. & Nott, D.L. (1980). A closer look at university student teacher supervision. Journal of Teacher Education. 30(4). 11-15.